THE SEARCH FOR TRANSCENDENCE

*the text of this book is printed
on 100% recycled paper*

THE SEARCH FOR TRANSCENDENCE

A THEOLOGICAL ANALYSIS OF NONTHEOLOGICAL ATTEMPTS TO DEFINE TRANSCENDENCE

WILLIAM A. JOHNSON

HARPER COLOPHON BOOKS
Harper & Row, Publishers
New York, Evanston, San Francisco, London

A hardcover edition is published by Harper & Row, Publishers, Inc.

THE SEARCH FOR TRANSCENDENCE.

Copyright © 1974 by William Alexander Johnson.

All rights reserved. Printed in the United States of America. No part of this book may
be used or reproduced in any manner without written permission except in the case of
brief quotations embodied in critical articles and reviews. For information address
Harper & Row, Publishers, Inc., 10 East 53rd Street, New York, N.Y. 10022. Published
simultaneously in Canada by Fitzhenry & Whiteside Limited, Toronto.

First HARPER COLOPHON edition published 1974.

LIBRARY OF CONGRESS CATALOG CARD NUMBER: 73–17607

STANDARD BOOK NUMBER: 06–090355–4 (PAPERBACK)

STANDARD BOOK NUMBER: 06–136133–X (HARDCOVER)

Designed by Ann Scrimgeour

PERFECTION
IS CREATED BY LIFE TRANSCENDING ITSELF.

—Stefan Zweig

CONTENTS

CHAPTER 3. TRANSCENDENCE AS *CREATIO EX NIHILO*
—R. D. LAING

CHAPTER 4. TRANSCENDENCE AS *FUTURE*
—ERNST BLOCH

CHAPTER 5. TRANSCENDENCE AS SELF-REALIZATION
—CARL G. JUNG

CONCLUSION. TOWARD A POSITIVE THEOLOGICAL
STATEMENT ON TRANSCENDENCE   148

PREFACE

The original theme for this book was suggested by the leaders and staff of the Episcopal Church conference, held in Berchtesgaden, Germany, in the spring of 1972. Much of the material embodied here was first expressed there and amplified and revised during a second Episcopal Church conference in the same city in the spring of 1973. I want to express formally my great appreciation to the participants of those conferences who, by gentle prodding and correction, enabled me to sharpen my ideas and to make them more intelligible to a larger audience. It is largely because of the good counsel and deliberate encouragement of Bishop Clarence E. Hobgood that these ideas were first expressed in Berchtesgaden and are now in print. I acknowledge my indebtedness to him for the many good associations I have developed because of the Berchtesgaden conferences, without at the same time implicating him in any of the errors and frailties of the material expressed in this book.

I want also to acknowledge the presence of the members of the Episcopal churches of the Convocation of Europe and especially the affectionate influence of Bishop Edmond Browning upon the ideas expressed in this book. And the clergy of St. Paul's American Episcopal Church in Rome, W. Charles Woodhams, Robert Pegram, and John Patterson, have heard many of these ideas expressed before and contributed heavily to their clarification.

Some of the ideas in this book will be familiar to my students at Manhattanville College and Brandeis University and to those good people who attended my classes at the Scarsdale Adult School and the Adult Class at the Church of St. James the Less, also in Scarsdale, New York.

I try to keep always in my mind, whenever I write or speak publicly, the presence of the Reverend Canon Edward N. West, who has always profoundly influenced my thinking and has contributed so concretely to my understanding of the historic Christian faith.

The manuscript was read in its entirety by Mrs. Madeleine L'Engle Franklin, my colleague at the Cathedral of St. John the Divine, who suggested many stylistic and substantive revisions. My wife, Carol Johnson, as always, has typed the manuscript several times, recommending changes and guiding it through the several steps toward its completion.

The Search for Transcendence is dedicated to Krister Frederick Johnson, who so often waited patiently while his father took too long to put his ideas on paper.

June 1973

THE SEARCH FOR
TRANSCENDENCE

INTRODUCTION

The search for transcendence is an absorbing and ongoing enterprise. Transcendence is the most discussed, the most compelling, and the most engaging of the subjects with which contemporary theologians deal. It is "where the theologian *is* at the moment." I would venture to argue that the search for transcendence is the most significant and valuable of all of those theological attempts to clarify the ancient faiths of Judaism and Christianity.[1]

However, the search for transcendence is not simply another one of those intellectual endeavors to resolve problems that no one is posing or to answer questions that no one is asking. The search is one which is prompted by the individual's search for a deeper and more profound meaning of life itself and for a sensitizing and intensification of human experience. The impulse to move from the ordinary dimensions of life to the extraordinary is not one invented by the theologian but is one which appears to spring up from the deepest levels of consciousness itself. Modern man recognizes that the superficiality and routineness of his ordinary, everyday life invites a profound reevaluation of that life. I am not suggesting that modern man thereupon seeks instinctively for metaphysical answers to personal problems, but I am arguing that he is competent to recognize the need for some resolution or amelioration or fulfillment of the deficiencies of his personal situation. Philip Slater proposed in his book *The Pursuit of Loneliness* that the more competent man becomes to master the complex world about him, the more necessary it is for man to search for human meaning within the depths of his own being. Robert Bellah, writing on the subject of "Transcendence in Contemporary Piety,"

1. Several examples of the literature of the search for transcendence are Peter L. Berger, *A Rumor of Angels: Modern Society and the Rediscovery of the Supernatural* (Garden City, N.Y.: Doubleday and Co., 1969); Herbert W. Richardson and Donald R. Cutler, eds., *Transcendence* (Boston: Beacon Press, 1961), which is a collection of addresses at a symposium on the subject of "Transcendence in Contemporary Culture" sponsored by the Church Society for College Work of Cambridge, Massachusetts.

argues that "the need to integrate the whole, known and unknown, conscious and unconscious, grows stronger. Somehow or other man must have a sense of the whole."[2] Bellah suggests that the symbols of transcendence become necessary for man in society in order for society to be capable of any creative and healthy activity. Transcendence offers unity amid the diversity and divisions of life; it offers courage in the face of uncertainty and unpredictability; it provides hope where all of the learned prognoses warrant only despair.

The search for transcendence, therefore, is not really an academic matter at all. It is more an underground concern which has been elevated to the level of sophisticated analysis. One does not have to encourage modern man to want to move from ordinary dimensions of action and consciousness to extraordinary dimensions of life. The flatness of life prompts the search. Everyone wants to participate in the search. The irritating and disjunctive divisions among the classes break down; the academician and the housewife seek for the same thing: some extra quality to life that gives meaning and hope and unity and inspiration.[3]

Transcendence is usually defined by the presence of "something above" or "something beyond" or "something more" than ordinary human experience. Whether transcendence is conceived of in a technical philosophical sense (as that metaphysical realm above the natural) or in an ordinary sense (as that phenomenon or experience found within the natural world but which appears to point beyond that world), the meaning is about the same. Many traditional theologians have conceived of the "something above" in spatial terms, and relegated the almighty, sovereign God to a place of habitation there. But the spate of popular theological books, inspired by the antimetaphysical posture of John A. T. Robinson, disabused many contemporary practitioners of the Jewish and Christian religions from ever again talking seriously about God "up there." God is rather described in terms of "the depth of being," symbolically referring to the way by

2. Quoted in Richardson and Cutler, *Transcendence,* p. 96.
3. Cf. Harvey Cox's essay "Feasibility and Fantasy: Sources of Social Transcendence" and his book *Feast of Fools,* both of which demonstrate the underground preoccupation with various forms of transcendence. Cf. also the recent best seller *Jonathan Livingston Seagull;* and also a more sophisticated analysis of the search, Theodore Roszak's *Where the Wasteland Ends* (Garden City, N.Y.: Doubleday, 1972).

which man orders his life about his relationship to the ultimate source of reality. And although the sophisticated academicians of that northeastern American theological beltway warn everyone of intellectual perfidy, the majority of practicing Jews and Christians, those pious folk who continue to frequent the holy places, affirm their faith (literally) in the God who, from vaulted heights, directs the affairs of men and empires.

But God's transcendence is prototypal in a magnanimous way. The notion of transcendence does not always necessitate the being of God to establish its veracity. Transcendence can also be related to a description of the humanistic objective of becoming something other than one is at present. As human beings, "we are never quite *there, we are always and deviously on the verge of being there.*"[4] The existentialists and the theology of hope devotees join in the chorus of ontologies of the "not yet completely being."

To sample a representative seeker for transcendence might be instructive at this introductory point. Huston Smith, who for many years has attempted to shed light for Western man on the ineluctable mysteries of the East, provides a valuable overview of the various possibilities of transcendence today.[5] He distinguishes between this-worldly transcendence and ontological transcendence, both of which are possible only when the condition of immanence is discounted. Immanence considers transcendence superfluous, finding inherent within human experience all of the conditions for total life fulfillment. Immanence seeks for nothing more. It is the best mode of life possible to man in this world. Life contains no inherent deficiencies. Transcendence is precluded as a possible experience because man has achieved the ends for which his life was created.[6] This-worldly transcendence is sought within the confines of reality as it is usually envisioned.

4. Philip Wheelwright, *The Burning Fountain* (Bloomington: Indiana University Press, 1968), p. 272.

5. Richardson and Cutler, *Transcendence,* pp. 1–17.

6. Wallace Stevens is quoted as a representative of the position which affirms the inherent perfection of immanence:

   . . . times of inherent excellence
  As when the cock crows on the left and all is well, incalculable balances,
  At which a kind of Swiss perfection comes.

Collected Poems (New York: Alfred A. Knopf, 1955), p. 786.

Smith describes specific human experiences or acts, characterized by their inherent human character. As such they are experiences or acts which cannot be delegated to supernatural or trans-human reality. Smith speaks of love, hope, and commitment to a cause as illustrative of this kind of transcendence. Love brings together diverse human beings and unites them in a sense of that which is eternal. At least the continuity engendered by two people in love gives the sense of an eternal relationship. Unity and eternalness are therefore the human attributes which fulfill the conditions of transcendence. Hope, in an ancillary way, unburdens the present, fills it with significance, and relates it to fulfillment and completion in the future. Hope thereby takes on a redemptive character. Commitment to a cause, too, fulfills the conditions of this-worldly transcendence because it allows the immediacy of one's ambitions to become subservient to longer range objectives; it subjects the narrowly conceived interests of an individual to the broader, more visionary goals of a community.

Ontological transcendence becomes necessary only when immanence and this-worldly transcendence do not function for the individual. This-worldly discontent is a requisite for ontological transcendence. Smith defines ontological transcendence as "that possibility that reality houses reservoirs of value qualitatively different from what we normally perceive or assume."[7] Ontological transcendence is that reality which exists "behind the scenes." Smith believes he can formulate conceptual forms for man's encounter with ultimate reality, that reality with which man's reason and imagination come into contact. He employs the concept of dimension to illustrate his point:

> The concept of a four-dimensional figure would, of course, apply to a physical object, animate or inanimate. But if we have gone this far, there is no need to stop. Living things might differ from the nonliving by their involvement in a fifth dimension. Death, then, would be the cessation of movement in the fifth dimension while the corpse continued its movement in the fourth. Spirit, as distinct from life alone, could be the product of a sixth dimension. A four-dimensional body would expand to a fifth dimension by being alive and to a sixth if it were evolving spiritually. Ample dimensions remain, of course, for God.[8]

7. Richardson and Cutler, *Transcendence,* p. 9.
8. Ibid., p. 14.

Smith opts for the viability of the search for ontological transcendence and is convinced that "reality includes surprising corridors of worth that elude ordinary eyes."

Peter Berger, a professional sociologist, has also devoted his conceptual energy to the search for transcendence. He begins with an anthropological starting point because the context for his search is within the empirically given human situation. It is just there that he discovers what he calls "signals of transcendence," or human experiences which point beyond the natural world of which the experiences are a part. Berger employs five arguments which satisfy his criterion of what he calls "prototypal human gestures." They point to the beyond in the midst of the ordinary and natural everyday awareness of man's orientation in time and space.

Berger's arguments are highly suggestive for the theologian searching for transcendence. This is especially so because Berger does not propound his arguments on the basis of a metaphysical, supernatural world "up there." Rather, he insists that there are certain kinds of distinctively human experiences, available to all men, which point specifically to the presence of the transcendent.

A. *The argument from ordering* presumes that man possesses a propensity for order, which ultimately is grounded in the faith that reality is as it should be. Berger does not argue that an empirical test can be devised to verify this faith. The assertion that there is an order in the universe must finally be an act of faith: "At the very center of the process of becoming fully human, at the core of *humanitas,* we find an experience of trust in the order of reality."[9]

B. *The argument from play* affirms that the individual, whether young or old, experiences transcendent qualities of liberation and joy through the act of playing. And furthermore, "in joyful play," as Berger would have it, "the time structure of the playful universe takes on a very specific quality—namely it becomes eternity."[10] The player steps out of time into the dimensions of eternity; he experiences joy as being and by so doing, suspends the chronological sequence of time.

C. *The argument from hope,* too, satisfies Berger's criteria for "sig-

9. Berger, *Rumor of Angels,* p. 69.
10. Ibid., p. 73.

nals of transcendence," which he argues are derivative of inductive faith. Inductive faith is faith derived from human experience, not from supernatural revelation. Man, Berger argues, cannot be adequately understood except in connection with his unquenchable capacity to hope for the future. And what Berger means specifically by man's capacity to hope is linked to particular acts which enhance rather than demean man's *humanitas*. These acts are, for Berger, "observable phenomena of the human situation whose intrinsic intention appears to be a deprecation or even denial of the reality of death."[11] They are therefore "signals of transcendence," and as such, indicators of a religious interpretation of reality.

D. *The argument from damnation* assumes that certain acts and experiences are so fundamentally inhuman that the only adequate response is one of absolute condemnation of the offense as well as the offender. Failure to do so would be not only a challenge to the sovereign character of justice but even more a "fatal impairment of *humanitas.*" Monstrously evil deeds are condemned prima facie by society. For example, the customary argument of the relative character of all human behavior becomes irrelevant when the deed is of the character of Eichmann's slaughter of the Jews in World War II. Berger writes:

> There are deeds that demand not only condemnation, but *damnation* in the full religious meaning of the word—that is, the doer not only puts himself outside the community of men; he also separates himself in a final way from a moral order that transcends the human community and thus invokes a retribution that is more than human.[12]

E. *The argument from humor* implies that humor is an essentially human phenomenon and is revelatory of the human situation. Humor identifies the comic element in all of life, and at the same time it relativizes the human condition: "At least for the duration of the comic perception, the tragedy of man is bracketed."[13] But humor also is an intimation of redemption; it is an experience which points to the possibility of liberation from the bondage of body and soul. And as such it is, for Berger, another signal of transcendence.

11. Ibid., p. 77.
12. Ibid., p. 84.
13. Ibid., p. 88.

Huston Smith and Peter Berger are illustrative of the contemporary search for transcendence. They have both demonstrated that the earnest seeker after transcendence may be rewarded for his efforts. But Smith and Berger are themselves committed personally and conceptually to the religious tradition of the Judaeo-Christian faith. They are in that sense apologists for religion. And although they do not identify themselves as professional dogmatic theologians of the Jewish and Christian faith traditions, they nonetheless offer powerful rational reasons why someone would want to make such an identification. Smith and Berger labor on the periphery of the academic theologian's sphere of influence; Smith among the natural scientists, Berger among the sociologists. But they labor successfully to demonstrate the intellectual viability of the committed Jew's and Christian's religious stance.

The essay which follows attempts to demonstrate that the search for transcendence also takes place among those detractors of a normative religion, represented in this case by Judaism and Christianity. What I intend to demonstrate is that transcendence is an objective sought by a number of thinkers whose primary field of activity is not the theological one. Furthermore, I want to argue that the nontheological attempts to discover secular transcendence are of significant value for the theologians of the Jewish and Christian faith traditions.

What I am suggesting is that the contemporary search for transcendence is a cross-disciplinary enterprise and that an interesting and methodologically valuable quest also takes place within the hallowed halls of the secular theorist. And it is that adversary of religious faith, he who would eschew any and all fellowship with the corps of theologians whose primary objective these days is to discover the transcendent, who can contribute significantly to the quest for transcendence. And I believe that I can demonstrate that the so-called secular definition of transcendence can function for the Jew and Christian as a corollary of or supplement to the definition with which he is now working. Or if that is too ambitious a proposal, I think I can at least demonstrate that the secular definition of transcendence possesses the capacity to enrich and invigorate the theological one. But what I want ultimately to argue is that the following illustrations of so-called secular definitions of transcendence contain what is already present within the Jewish and Christian understanding of transcendence, especially when those definitions are aware of the biblical configurations of transcendence. For that reason, a minimal definition of transcendence for the Jew and Christian ought to contain those definitions of transcendence proposed by Charles Reich (transcendence as personal liberation), Herbert Marcuse (transcendence as the possibility of historical alternative), R. D. Laing (transcendence as *creatio ex nihilo*), Ernst Bloch (transcendence as future), and Carl G. Jung (transcendence as self-realization).

1

TRANSCENDENCE AS PERSONAL LIBERATION —CHARLES REICH

A. EXPOSITION

1. THE CONCEPT OF TRANSCENDENCE

The concept of transcendence is the key to Reich's now well-known description of Consciousness III. With almost evangelical fervor he writes: "Consciousness III is an attempt to gain transcendence. . . . It seeks restoration of the nonmaterial elements of man's existence, the elements like the natural environment and the spiritual that were passed by in the rush of material development. It seeks to transcend science and technology, to restore them to their proper place as tools of man rather than as determinants of man's existence. . . . It makes the wholly rational assertion that machines should do the bidding of man, of man who knows and respects his own nature and the natural order of which he is a part. The new consciousness seeks new ways to live in light of what technology has made both possible and desirable. Since machines can produce enough food and shelter for all, why should not man end the antagonism derived from scarcity and base his society on love for his fellow-man? If machines can take care of our material wants, why should not man develop the aesthetic and spiritual side of his nature."[1]

Reich's analysis of the American consciousness during the course

---

1. Charles Reich, *The Greening of America* (New York: Random House, 1970), pp. 351–352.

of the last one hundred years is an intriguing and provocative one and focuses directly on the concept of transcendence as the means by which America can transform the brutalized society created by Consciousness I and II. There are three general types of consciousness in America:

Consciousness I, the consciousness of the nineteenth century farmer and small entrepreneur, working hard individually to get ahead;

Consciousness II, the consciousness of the corporate state, the new organizational society, that new society created by the liberal reformists of the New Deal;

Consciousness III, the consciousness of the new generation, of the young person who has seen the vision of how to transcend the "contradictions, failures and exigencies of the Corporate State itself " and who accomplishes this vaunted goal not by direct political means but by changing culture and the quality of individual lives. Consciousness III is itself the catalyst which will convert all of American society to a different course to effect the revolution of all of the structures of American society.

Reich has learned well the lesson that Marx taught a century and a half ago in the emerging industrialized Europe, that man's spiritual and aesthetic condition is *derivative* of his work, that is, that man's most human characteristics are molded by what he does during his workday. It is Reich's contention that Marx's thesis, when writ large, when man is conditioned not simply by the environment of his work but by a culture or a culture-consciousness (which controls the political and economic machine), the consequence is a man devoid of basic human qualities. Man is then a "hollow man," alienated from his work as he is alienated from basic human needs. Reich invites his readers to look at the faces of America to verify his assertion: the man waiting for a commuter train, the man eating in a government cafeteria, the career woman who has lost her beauty. Work has devastated these people. And these same people have devastated their land and their waterways.

A sober picture, but I believe an accurate one. It is important to recognize the centrality of the concept of transcendence in Reich's attempt to resolve the dilemma of the modern (that is, Consciousness II) American. What I think is less satisfactory and incorrect is Reich's identification of transcendence with the empirical presence of so-called liberated students, who among other activities smoke marijuana and wear long hair. "Long hair . . . has crossed all barriers; no one has fought it successfully. Can anyone doubt that it will reach all the men in our society within a few years?"[2] That kind of cultural optimism is hardly of the variety which warrants the optimism that the entire spiritual life of contemporary American man will be transformed. I do not believe that subsequent historical events in the United States have substantiated Reich's thesis, nor do I believe that the revolution that Reich predicted has come about. Nor do I believe that it will come according to the scenario he has proposed. But more of that later. I think it necessary to remind the reader of the major facets of Reich's argument and of some of his important concepts and also to see where Reich's ideas are shaped by his mentors in revolutionary strategy: Marx, Marcuse, Polanyi, Ellul, Mailer, Kesey, and others.

The most crucial notion with which Reich is dealing is the notion of consciousness itself. Somewhat akin to the *Weltanschauung* philosophers of the nineteenth century—Hegel, Fichte, and Schelling—Reich uses the term consciousness to mean man's total configuration of his own particular reality. "Consciousness is not a set of opinions, information, or values, but a total configuration in any given individual, which makes up his whole perception of reality, his whole world view."[3] Man's consciousness is socially determined, particularly if man has allegiance to Consciousness I or Consciousness II. There is for Reich a unity of consciousness which includes man's beliefs, understanding, and values, his response to the possibility of change (acceptance, resistance), his education, his political affiliations, and his emotional responses. But consciousness is more than all of these, it is man's "head," his way of life. "It is that by which he creates his own life and thus creates the society in which he lives."[4]

Consciousness as a mass phenomenon is formed as a construct from the underlying economic and social conditions of man, from his cul-

2. Ibid., pp. 330–331.
3. Ibid., p. 14.
4. Ibid., p. 16.

ture and his government. One contributes to the stability and functionality of the other; for example, if one is committed to the free
enterprise system, then government's adoption of laissez faire economics corroborates one's consciousness. Disfunctionality and insta-
bility come about when consciousness and social and political practices do not square with one another. Reich looks at the development
of consciousness as part of a coherent pattern of history. Beneath the
chaos in our society, the utter meaninglessness of political events, the
continued brutalization of urban man and black man, the endless
repetition of death and more death in Southeast Asia, the lack of
heroes able to rally a people about a principle of national righteousness, and underneath man's impotence to change historical events,
there is, Reich argues, a power at work to effect a revolution in
American life, a quiet revolution which "will originate with the individual and with culture, and it will change the political structure as
its final act."[5] Therefore the epochs of change in the history of the
United States are constructs of a changing American consciousness.

2. THE ANTECEDENT CONSCIOUSNESS OF AMERICA

Consciousness I is the consciousness of the new American, the immi-
grant, the individual who was promised a new way of life and a new
form of government in which people would be sovereign. It is characterized by an individualism in which man was freed from aged Euro-
pean class distinctions. It meant the end of social meritocracies and
a chance to achieve for oneself and to fulfill oneself. The American
dream was one which counted human dignity as a primary virtue and
which valued equality because of the spiritual unity of all people
within the American community.

What happened to the primitive innocence of the American was
that self-interest and competitiveness corrupted his character. He no
longer trusted his neighbor but looked at him rather as someone
capable of undercutting him in his business dealings. Aggression soon
replaced the so-called spiritual unity of the American community.
Success, measured in terms of wealth and the capacity to consume,

5. Ibid., p. 4.

became the overriding motive of the American. Narrowly defined notions of self-interest became the determinative factor of the new American character, or, in Reich's terms, "the American consciousness."

Concomitant to the fall from innocence was Consciousness I's inability to allow for change in the social and economic and political structures that determined man's life. Consciousness I demonstrated thereby a resistance to cultural change. But it continued to believe that the American dream was possible and that the virtues of hard work and self-discipline led in a providential manner to success. Among the members of Consciousness I, Reich includes the American farmers, owners of small businesses, immigrants who retain their sense of nationality, conservative AMA types, many members of Congress, gangsters, Republicans, and "just plain folks."[6] Reich does not deny that such an aggregate of Americans has a morality which motivates their behavior. But it is a morality based upon individual rather than social righteousness, upon good will rather than upon visible social consequences; a morality which promises a return to the simplistic life of the frontier where men were men and the best government was that which governed least. It is a morality based upon allegiance to law and order, but one which is defined by the powerful politicians in league with the industrialists; a new legalism which advocates "strict constitutionality," but which usually intends the exclusion of progressive and liberal interpretations of the Constitution.

Consciousness II is the expression of the concerted effort on the part of some people in America to reform the way of life which created the economic and social chaos of the nineteenth century. People began to seek governmental reform to lead America into the real world of the twentieth century. The troubles of the nineteenth century were caused by the evils of unlimited competition and the abuses brought about by those with economic power. Laws were passed which effected reform: laws which regulated child labor and stopped unhealthy practices in the meat markets; the prohibition of monopolies; laws against unbridled competition in some industries such as banking

6. Ibid., pp. 25–26.

and the railroads; the regulation of working conditions for certain industries; and laws against dishonest advertising. The government was the reforming agent. The government determined what kinds of economic practices were against the "public interest" and passed laws to prohibit their continued practice. The populist and progressive Wilsonian era and the New Deal were the chief protagonists of this revision in the American consciousness. The American reform movement was committed to the regulation of the abuses of capitalism and to the redistribution of power within society. The recognition of the labor movement and the initiation of governmental economic planning were its chief accomplishments.

What occurred, however, as a result of New Deal and other progressive measures was the creation of a "public state," which matched the power of and had the capability to regulate the private corporate state. Regulatory legislation created new governmental agencies. The executive branch of the government was expanded. The public state functioned well when it managed and administered, for the "public interest," the various operations of the corporate state. The New Deal produced a kind of elitist society, in which power was transferred from the man in the street to the man in government. The New Deal, with all of its achievements in the administration of government, did not understand the problems of the loss of human meaningfulness, the loss of the sense of community and self, and the final dehumanization of the environment.[7]

Consciousness II accompanied the New Deal reformist developments. Consciousness II saw an America where organization was dominant. The individual was sacrificed to the effectively functioning organization. The system and the power resident within the system became the dominant factors of man's conception of reality. There was no life for the individual by himself. He could not survive without the system.

Reich gathers together a diverse group within Consciousness II, including new-style businessmen, liberal intellectuals, educated professionals and technicians, middle-class suburbanites, labor union leaders, the Eugene McCarthy supporters, blue collar workers with

7. Ibid., p. 52.

newly purchased homes, old-line leftists, and members of the Communist party USA.[8] The rallying cry for Consciousness II was liberalism and reform. It meant greater commitment of the individual to the public interest and more social responsibility by private business. But above all, it meant governmental regulation and control, the creation of a managed welfare state. It intended the reform of the evils created by Consciousness I: racial prejudice, isolationism, narrowly defined social goals, and misplaced economic priorities. Consciousness II was optimistic about man's ability to improve society by the creative use of technology and by organization and by social manipulation. The individual had to sacrifice his personal values to those of the organization. "The Consciousness II man thus adopts, as his *personal* values, the structure of standards and rewards set by his occupation or organization."[9] Consciousness II, according to Reich, denied the uniqueness of individuals; it sorted people out in terms of standards of classification and according to the ways by which they could be dealt with effectively within the organization. It judged individuals according to generalized institutional standards. Furthermore, there was built into Consciousness II a very rigid meritocracy which "permitted" the individual to do only what the organization allowed. "Consciousness II is in favor of many reforms, but he will not jeopardize his own status to fight for them; he will not put his own body on the line."[10]

Herbert Marcuse, in *One Dimensional Man,* documents much of Reich's analyses. Marcuse's criticism is that the state which administers most effectively is that state which manipulates consciousness. The state does so by influencing the culture and environment which impinge upon man's consciousness of himself. The result is a bogus understanding of the self, a self upon which false needs have been imposed by society. The "authentic self" is therefore administered and the individual acts out of a false sense of reality.

Consciousness II, in Reich's analysis, has brutalized man so that motives of power and success and status and achievement become the

8. Ibid., p. 66.
9. Ibid., p. 73.
10. Ibid., p. 77.

criteria for humanization. But with it comes the loss of "dread, awe, wonder, mystery, accidents, failures, helplessness, magic." Consciousness II has destroyed man's search for the self and has created a society that prohibits man from any authentic questing after meaningfulness.[11]

3. THE NATURE OF CONSCIOUSNESS III

Consciousness III comes about as a consequence of a government that is not effectively flexible, sophisticated, or able to understand what needs to be done to effect a significant humanistic revolution. The power of the state lies in its ability to maintain false social objectives. But now the power resident within the state has begun to destroy itself. Reich discovers all sorts of incipient rebellions within the social fabric of the United States: organized consumer dissatisfactions, a consumer-worker contradiction, commuter refusal to pay fares, local school boards objecting to the quality of education that the children receive, increased criticism of false advertising, worker rebellion, dissatisfaction with jobs, strikes by municipal employees, and ghetto riots. Lawlessness is the major motif of the breakdown of American society. It can be seen foremost in youth's criticism of the war in Vietnam but also in the tendency on the part of young people to "steal whenever they can get away with it." Both acts are indicative of young people's refusal to accept "the system" any longer, their rejection of the massive corporate state and the establishment and the military-industrial complex. The war, however, was the agent which forced a major breach in consciousness. "It rent the fabric of consciousness so drastically as to make repair almost impossible. And it made a gap in belief so large that through it people could begin to question the other myths of the Corporate State."[12]

Consciousness III emerged out of the arid ground of Consciousness II. It appeared to take the form of an organized conspiracy. It was made possible, Reich argues, by two interacting forces: one, the promise made to all Americans of an affluent life; and two, the threat to that life by the impoverishment of the spirit witnessed to by the war in Vietnam, the false glitter of commercialism, and the real fear of the

11. Ibid., p. 141.
12. Ibid., p. 216.

destruction of all of life by the nuclear holocaust. The children of middle-class affluent America refused to buy the false myths of their parents' attitudes, values, and manner of living, expressed so often by such messages as "don't live the way we have, don't settle for the emptiness of our lives, don't be lured by the things we valued, don't neglect life and love as we have."[13]

Young people listened to James Joyce and Wallace Stevens and Salinger's Holden Caulfield and Eldridge Cleaver and Malcolm X and rock music; they smoked pot and let their hair grow longer. A subculture, a counterculture grew up of young people "converted" to the new consciousness. "The foundation of Consciousness III is liberation. It comes into being the moment the individual frees himself from automatic acceptance of the imperatives of society and the false consciousness which society imposes."[14] Liberation has to do with the individual freedom to create a philosophy of life for oneself, to build one's own values and live according to one's own life-style, but ultimately to create a culture for oneself and for all men. The individual self, Reich argues again and again, is the primary reality of Consciousness III. Not allegiance to a party or an organization, nor imprisonment within a profession or the corporate state, nor an acceptance of the public interest can be authentic motives for true human life.

The character of Consciousness III can be summarized as follows:

a. One never does violence to oneself; that is, one never allows oneself to become a means toward an end.

b. One is never alienated from the self. "Be true to oneself," which means "to start from premises based on human life and the rest of nature, rather than premises that are the artificial products of the Corporate State, such as power or status."[15]

c. One lives completely for each moment, never deferring meaning to the future.

d. One postulates the absolute worth of every human self. "People are brothers, the world is ample for all."

e. One rejects the concept of excellence and comparative merit.

f. One refuses to evaluate people by general standards, refuses to

13. Ibid., p. 221.
14. Ibid., p. 225.
15. Ibid.

classify them or even to analyze them. One rejects all kinds of merito-cracies and hierarchies of value.

g. One is honest in all human relationships and will never use another person. "Be wholly honest with others, use no other person as a means."

h. One does not alter oneself for someone else's sake. "By being one's true self one offers others the most; one offers them something honest, genuine, and more important, something for them to respond to, to be evoked by."

i. One values loyalty, not artificial duty.

j. One is suspicious of "obligations" and contractual relations be-tween people.

And there is much more. But the general notion of what makes up Consciousness III ought now to be clear. The consequence of this consciousness is a radical critique of society. But it is not a critique of society based upon a sophisticated program for revolution from the strategies of Marx or Marcuse. It is rather a rejection of the values and attitudes and behavior of Consciousness II. Consciousness III simply begins from premises different from those of Consciousness II. It rejects the untruthful and unhealthy and hypocritical society that it sees not because of grand ideological insights about the nature of society but because of its artificiality and inherent destructiveness. Consciousness III, therefore, begins from a different set of values from Consciousness I and Consciousness II. Consciousness III is reformist not because of a commitment to a specific plan of reform as the Kennedy liberal would suggest. He is committed to reform because only with reform can the welfare of the individual be magnified. He is responsible for the remolding of society, but he "puts his body on the line." When powerless in the decision-making process, responsi-bility demands that he gain such power.[16]

Reich believes that the fashions and dress of young people are specific indices of the new consciousness. He believes that blue jeans and bell-bottoms are outward and visible signs of the new-found enthusiasm, spontaneity, happiness, and freedom of a large segment of our society. The freedom regarding clothes, too, expresses "a

16. Ibid., p. 232.

wholeness of self against the schizophrenia of Consciousness II." The new clothes are inexpensive, they allow for work and play, and they also allow for imaginative differences within the drab browns, greens, and blues. They are earthy and sensual and allow for mobility in all sorts of social activities. Clothes make it possible for people to be honest and natural with one another. As well, they express the shared values of youth and are therefore expressive of the new consciousness.

In essence, according to Reich, Consciousness III is the recovery of the self. The youth who embraces Consciousness III has stepped outside of the system; his goals have radically changed. "The new concept gives rise to a new freedom: with one idea of himself a man would feel ridiculously self-conscious wearing bell-bottoms; he is a banker or lawyer making a fool of himself. But if he thought of himself as a person with a sense of humor he would feel at home in clothes with a lighter touch; he would have that new freedom. Thus the world is no longer bleak, because the individual has discovered that within his own creative ability lies the power to transform it."[17] And so it is with Reich; Consciousness III has rediscovered the true meaning of the self and with it a new knowledge of reality!

Reich describes transcendence as personal liberation or redemption. He wants man to get back to the authentic sources of his being. Youth leads the way, but older people can rediscover the true self too. And this can mean the recovery of self from the mass of duties and obligations and fears and external standards which have up to the point of conversion destroyed man's authentic self. The recovery of self is nothing less than the recapturing of life itself. There is also included within Reich's revolutionary schema the task of the new generation to teach others the way to rediscover the self, "so that the great liberating process of recovery of self, started by our youth, can become the means of liberation for all Americans."[18] The religious connotation fits perfectly into the "conversion" motif described earlier.

Reich describes the agony of American society in personalistic and attitudinal terms. He is fond of alluding to Mailer's *The Naked and*

17. Ibid., p. 271.
18. Ibid., p. 295.

the Dead, which showed that the source of war is in the barren and impoverished lives that Americans lead. War, as an institutional and political struggle, is inevitable because of the aggression and hostility engendered in the lives of Americans by society itself. Once personal attitudes change, then the kinds of institutional structures which permit wars will never again be possible.

The attempts in the past to alter attitudes have failed. Christianity, for example, Reich maintains, has asked man to give up power, aggression, and materialism for a promise of something better in another world. Christianity offered a change, but a remote one, not a real one. However, Consciousness III offers a change that is immediate, real, sensual, loving, and liberating. It encourages the individual to "listen to music, dance, seek out nature, laugh, be happy, be beautiful, help others whenever you can, work for them as best you can, take them in, the old and bitter as well as the young, live fully in each moment, love and cherish each other, love and cherish yourselves, stay together."[19]

Reich's notion of transcendence as personal liberation offers much which is instructive to Jews and Christians.

B. ANALYSIS AND CRITIQUE

1. CONSCIOUSNESS III AND REDEMPTION

Reich's concept of Consciousness III means much the same as Jews and Christians have meant by redemption, that is, the individual's discovery of the authentic self, which is created and sustained by the sovereign and almighty God.

But what must be criticized is Reich's identification of the empirically redeemed man with Consciousness III. All men, including the liberated youth in America, share the same human situation, participate in the same human impoverishment, and stand before the same potentialities for human development. Reich's analysis of the agonies of America is deficient just at that point where he claims to have discovered some authentic development within the human spirit. As

19. Ibid., p. 347.

he designates one group of Americans, out of the totality of the whole human race, and elevates them to a position of greater awareness of what it means to be human, he is in error. By so doing, Reich excludes a group of people from the existential advantage of standing in judgment before a Sovereign Being, or a transcendent criterion, or whatever you want to call a standard of fulfilled humanity. The beings who make up Reich's Consciousness III then become either tyrants, whose behavior and ambitions are absolutized, or dumb animals, who have exhausted completely what it means for man to be human. Without some goal of perfection or purity or greater duty and commitment or the supreme height of feeling and experience, the man whom Reich describes becomes easily satisfied with himself and an easy prey for hedonistic enslavement. Without the image of what it might mean to *become* human or to be human as humanity has been attained by someone else, a hero in culture, for example, Consciousness III becomes pedestrian and provincial beyond belief. But Reich allows for this basic error in the creation of the new humanity because, as he argues, the immediacy of man's experience is somehow indicative of the profoundest moment in cosmic history. To do so is to elevate man to the level of the angels and never to allow him to stand in judgment by a transcendent standard which insists upon greater achievement in the quest for a fulfilled humanity.

Reich calls for transcendence, for the creation of the new being, the truly human being, man who is liberated from the crass and materialistic environment within which his parents and his government have placed him. But he makes the error of identifying that new creature with one particular cultural development present in the United States today, that is, the emergence of a unique and distinguishable youth culture. By so doing, Reich has committed the fallacy of the domestication of the notion of transcendence, and any neophyte in the Jewish or Christian traditions could have told Reich that he was totally wrong.

2. REICH'S CLASSIFICATORY CRITERIA

Reich builds into his classificatory criteria a means to deter his readers from any criticism of his fundamental assumptions. It is difficult to criticize his assumptions, for if you do so, you can only do so from the perspectives of Consciousness I or Consciousness II. Consciousness III, however, is above criticism. One is either a part of the new consciousness or is still imprisoned in a past and antiquated and self-destructive vision of what it means to be human. Reich labels you in an absolute way. If you disagree with him, you belong to another consciousness, and you could not possibly understand the new spirit of freedom which is abroad in the land. Psychologically what Reich's classifications have done is to introduce an intellectual totalitarianism into his view of humanity. If you belong to Consciousness III, you are right; if you don't, you are mistaken or out of touch. Reich would encourage you to come on board Consciousness III. But should you not want to, for all sorts of reasons, such as age, temperament, or sensitivity to different music and fashion, or because you believe that Reich's analysis is wrong and that there is no revolution in the land and that it could be effected least of all by the young people of America, then Reich, according to his own criteria, can only label you as in error and less than human and ultimately a lost soul.

Such classificatory criteria are to my mind not simply trite, they introduce into other attempts at revolutionary change a divisive note, forcing someone to locate himself within prescribed standards of revolutionary consciousnesses. Reich introduces into society the element which he has avowed to remove: division of individuals into classes. Individuals are now differentiated according to their acceptance or rejection of Reich's thesis.

However, Reich would claim that such a judgment misses the point. And that is because one cannot discuss Consciousness III analytically or systematically.[20] By so doing, one engages in an intellectual process which Consciousness III automatically rejects. But I want to insist that you cannot exclude analytical thought from intellectual constructions. No ideology or revolutionary mood or liberated consciousness is so sacrosanct that it cannot be subject to some hard-nosed questioning as to its basic premises. Reich has given an aristocratic status to his thesis.

20. Ibid., p. 224.

3. THE FUNDAMENTAL ANACHRONISM OF REICH'S
REVOLUTIONARY CONSCIOUSNESS

Reich's revolution in consciousness is both empirically and historically anachronistic; that is, it has not worked in our society. I am sure
that the most valid judgment one can make of Reich's Consciousness
III is that it has not effected a visible and real change in American
society. Peter Berger, in his critique of *The Greening of America,*
insists that the basic social drive in the USA is still toward the middle
class, in which the motives of success and achievement and acquisi-
tiveness and consumption are fundamental human characteristics.
What has really changed? Has the fashion industry given up the ghost
in response to the common uniforms worn by today's youth? Not at
all; the challenge to the industry has been vigorously accepted, and
new and creative ways have been devised to get middle-class affluent
American youth to change the color of their jeans, to add brocade to
their gypsy jerseys, and to purchase a used (but still attractive and
functional) leather coat with beaver lining for colder weather. The
phonograph record industry has reaped a fortune from the members
of the new consciousness, as have the motor scooter and automobile
manufacturers. What Reich does not know is that life styles change
according to historically and socially determined forces and that they
are derivative of these forces. What this means is nothing more than
that Consciousness III is a direct result of a concerted effort (one
might call it "a conspiracy") on the part of the corporate state, the
powerful leaders of industry and government, to assuage the potentially disruptive character of an abnormally large youth culture into
impotent and antirevolutionary behavior. The social behavior of our
youth has indeed changed, but it has been changed by the architects
of America's public behavior and changed so that it cannot disrupt
the established status quo. Human behavior does not change, as Reich
would suggest, by some invisible historical revolutionary force. Behavior changes as the culture manipulators and the taste makers join
forces with governmental agencies (who want the populace to behave
in a particular way) to create a docile people and an impotent populace. Changes have not taken place in the location of power in govern-

ment. In fact, power has not been challenged at all. And it is Consciousness III which encourages its adherents not to become involved in power. Political power is antihuman. It can only pervert the soul's quest for authenticity. But the fact is that ultimately political power devours those who refuse to attempt to manipulate it for humanistic objectives.

What I am suggesting is that there is no great change in the consciousness of the American youth. He drops out for a time, but only temporarily, and then rejoins his confreres within the middle-class subculture, struggling to achieve the same objectives that his parents attempted to achieve a generation earlier.

4. THE POLITICAL NAIVETE OF REICH'S POSITION

Reich's program takes the individual out of the American political structures by asserting that they are not worthy of human involvement. Consciousness III does this in two ways: first, by denying that power, of the corporate state, of the establishment, even of the liberal party, is of any ultimate significance in the human struggle; and second, by the optimistic posture that power will ultimately be thwarted by spiritual forces resident within the human soul or heart or psyche. Reich is inviting his adherents to become consciously and deliberately nonpolitical beings, that is, to become impotent within the American body politic. Drop out of the system, he advises, and the remarkable consequence will be that the system will change!

Furthermore, Reich's reformist program is full of inconsistencies. He describes the relationship of the individual to the society he is attempting to reform in the chapter on "The New Generation." The individual, Reich asserts, is that reality which does not accept the goals or standards of society. But he recognizes that "society has a vast influence on the welfare of people everywhere." The influence of society is detrimental. But for the welfare of individuals, Reich is committed to the improvement of society. But why? Why should he want to change society if it is inherently evil and if its conception of reality is wrong? Why can he not draw the logical conclusion that he, too, is a product of society and that he has shared in its benefits and failures and therefore has a moral responsibility to change it? Why drop out of it? Why should one get out and let society go to hell?

No, what Reich has done is to reject society in favor of the individual. But he recognizes finally that the individual needs society for individual self-fulfillment. But Reich cannot have it both ways. He has chosen the individual. Then he cannot have society to fulfill individual needs.

Reich has created the ideological raison d'être for an entire generation of human beings to be overwhelmed by those in political power. The extraordinary meaning in Reich's counsel is that for him to be free means to be liberated from the American political system. The irony in all of this is that Reich wants contemporary man to be free but then establishes instead the means for his enslavement. And enslavement occurs not accidentally, nor by the conquest of a stronger opposing power, but by the conscious abandonment of political involvement by young people. The youth of America become politically impotent because it has been mandated that it is beneath their spiritual dignity to become involved.

What then is the consequence? First, the American political machine proceeds without representation from one major segment of American life, its young people. Legislation reflects other interests, values, attitudes than those expressed by the young. The American political establishment thereby expresses a functional disenfranchisement, not, however, because powerful groups in the legislature have excluded young people, but rather because Consciousness III has advocated that it should be so.

Second, in many subtle ways, legislation is enacted which tyrannizes young people and does so specifically in terms of their potential for freedom and their ability to say and act and dress in the way they want. Social progress thereby excludes the young person's opportunity to express his convictions regarding the war, ecology, the problems of race and the ghettos, and so on. Disenfranchisement has the consequence of discriminating against the life styles, attitudes, and ambitions (and ultimately the consciousness) of young people.

Third, a part of the American electorate eschews any ideological identification with the significant political, social, and cultural developments taking place in the United States. For example, the same students who supported Eugene McCarthy in 1968 because he offered a viable ideological option to the establishment postures of the Republican and Democratic parties were able to support James Buckley in the New York senatorial election because he, too, appeared to offer a different variety of political position. But to be able to do so is clearly to miss the most important point of American political life, that is, that power is the consequence of ideology and he who would want to develop humanistic programs for social change must first be elected to political office. And Buckley is different ideologically from McCarthy; and Buckley has power and McCarthy has none. Which means simply that Buckley's brand of political ideology will expand throughout the United States, while McCarthy's will not. Reich is leading his followers down the primrose path to political meaninglessness!

5. REICH'S ANTIREVOLUTIONARY CONSCIOUSNESS

Consciousness III cannot be conceived of as a revolution at all. When one speaks of revolution, one conceives of cadres of dedicated professionals who devote themselves totally to the vision of a world radically altered by social and political change. Lenin's sacrifices for the cause of the Bolshevik revolution come to mind immediately. Lenin in Zurich preparing himself for the call to come to the Finland Station in St. Petersburg represents a different consciousness entirely from the immediacy and lack of discipline of Reich's revolutionaries.

The revolutionary Commune in Paris established in March of 1871, which Marx called a "thunderburst," the brave uprising by the citizenry of the French capital, has little to do with today's communes experimenting in group living. The Commune in 1871 meant wresting away from the government the power to govern themselves on a local level; it meant decentralization and municipal and local liberty. It was "all power to the people." It was the political form of the Commune that impressed Marx. Paris was simply claiming its municipal rights and the right of local government. It affirmed the sovereign power of the people, particularly the workers. One poet expressed the faith of the Commune with these words:

> They can kill us, if they wish, they can rip down our posters and remove all traces from the walls, but the principles that have been affirmed will

still exist, and whatever is done, whatever is said, they are monuments
that the Versaillais cannot destroy either by strokes of the pen or shots
of the gun.[21]

Reich's revolution is a sham revolution; it is a call to effect change
without any change in the political structures which determine the
will and destiny of man. It is a call to a revolution with no visible signs
of political alignment, no defiance of stated political authority, no
sacrifice for principles, no self-discipline, and what is ultimately most
absurd, it is a revolution without ideology.

But it is easy to discover the roots of Reich's antirevolutionism, that
is, his refusal to accept the attempts on the part of "true liberals" (as
he calls them) to bring about changes in the political establishment
in political and legal ways. Reich claims that those attempts have not
been fruitful.[22] But have they not been? Has not legislation changed
the status of the black man in America, even if that change has been
a minimal one in terms of voting rights and antilynch laws? The point
is, I think, that the power controlled by the white man in America
has begun to be wrested away by the black man. And that has come
about through legal and extralegal means. But it is only a token to be
sure, and much needs yet to be done. However, what is the alternative? I cannot see that there is any. Social and political change comes
about before there is a change in consciousness. Reich believes that
society can change as the hearts of its members are changed. Such a
notion did not work historically for the Moral Rearmament Movement, and it will not work for Reich either. One changes the structures of government, then one can work to effect a change in human
consciousness.

Reich somewhere talks about the "conversion" of the parents of
runaway draft evaders, those solid conservative types, whose point of
view is radically altered when their own sons protest their nation's
participation in Vietnam. My experience shows too many instances of
parents who disown their children, "washing their hands" of their
wayward progeny. Rather than a conversion experience, there is a

21. Steward Edwards, "Paris Burns Behind Its Barricades," *The Critic,* Vol. xxx
(Nov.–Dec., 1971): 35–39.
22. Reich, *Greening of America,* pp. 315 ff.

hardening of the parents' position. And what is most tragic, a brutalizing rupture has torn apart the family unit! The case of the Berrigan brothers has been instructive on this point. Rather than the creation of solidarity within the family, members of the family have denounced the "unpatriotic and tyrannous" behavior of their priest-brothers.

6. THE UTOPIANISM WITHIN REICH'S POSITION

Implicit within Reich's notion of Consciousness III is a superficial and stupid utopianism, a commitment to a nineteenth century romanticism that cannot square with the political realities of the twentieth century.[23] Reich writes, "If we want peace but still believe that countries with differing ideologies are threats to one another, we will not get peace."[24] But what Reich does not seem to grasp is the fact that nations are real political and military threats to one another, that no united world community has ever been established, and that in this world such a community could never come into being. The national sovereignty of one nation by definition comes into conflict with that of another. Communities are not created by fiat, Reinhold Niebuhr once said, and world communities are illusions, romantic dreams which can never be corroborated with historical facts.

Reich believes that Consciousness III will do away with wars, but he also believes that conservation, auto safety, and hospital care can be achieved by a change in consciousness.[25] "The machine can be controlled at the "consumer" level only by people who change their whole value system." But surely no change in value systems is possible without a change in those socio-economic structures which create consumers and consumer needs. That obvious point, which both Karl

23. One is readily aware of Reich's more than average middle-class tastes and values. Cf. Chapter VI, "The Lost Self," in which Reich lists his own preferences for human experience: eg., *Adventure, Travel*—"The Yukon, the Hebrides, a blizzard, fog on the Grand Banks, the lost cities of Crete, climbing a mountain on rock and ice in elemental cold and wind." (p. 152) That hardly represents a list of possible human experiences for someone who does not belong to a highly professional, financially comfortable, well-traveled, sophisticated, self-assured class of individuals. Yet Reich claims a "greening of America" which is to become universal, the benefits of which are to become available to all.

24. Reich, *The Greening of America,* p. 317.

25. Ibid.

Marx and Vance Packard have affirmed, seems to have evaded Reich's whole intellectual perspective.

Reich's utopianism is clearly not of a moderate variety:

> When the new consciousness has achieved its revolution and rescued us from destruction, it must go about the task of learning how to live in a new way. . . . The new way of life proposes a concept of work in which quality, dedication, and excellence are preserved, but work is nonalienated, is the free choice of every person, is integrated into a full and satisfying life, and expresses and affirms each individual being.[26]

No one, even in the wildest dreams of the Victorian attempt to create the kingdom of God on earth, conceives of Reich's revolution as a possible human achievement. In fact, Reich's description of the completely nonartificial and nonalien community sounds to me something like the medieval description of heaven.

Marx, in his *Economic and Philosophical Manuscripts of 1844*, envisaged a society in which man would be creatively related to his work, but he could promise such a society only after the proletariat revolution had been achieved. Reich's proposals effect no revolution. The proletariat is never freed from tyranny. The proletariat is, for Reich, never identifiable as such. And when the workers are identified, they are relegated to Consciousness II, thereby vitiating their ability to grasp the true nature of the change warranted by our society.

7. THE NONFUNCTIONAL CHARACTER OF REICH'S POSITION

Not much more need be said. But I am obliged to speak too of the nonfunctionality of Reich's consciousness schema. It simply does not work. Consciousness III is not changing the world. No revolution is coming into being. But what is more, it is impossible to convince anyone of the viability of Reich's plans for world revolution. How can one introduce Consciousness III as a live option to a fifteen-year-old, for example? And here I'm reacting to Reich as a parent. Reich instructs all American youth to affirm that parents are wrong, they are misguided liberals, they belong to the corporate state, and they are dehumanized to the point where they do not know what it means to

26. Ibid., p. 19.

be human any longer. He tells the youth of America that their natural disaffection for their parents is not misguided. He argues that the young person is right simply by virtue of the fact that he is young! He ought to reject his parents. Parents represent tyrannical authority and totalitarian supremacy. What they say is necessarily inadequate and downright wrong!

But such counsel can only come from a social dilettante who recognizes no immediate responsibility for family life and parental concern for children. What I conceive to be the task of parents is to prepare their children to leave their homes but to do so graciously, with impunity, but prepared for what they themselves conceive to be the meaning of adulthood. But that means they will be equipped psychologically and emotionally to achieve full humanity for themselves in an alien and unlovely world. But that also presupposes parental guidance and attention to open up vistas for art and travel and physical expression, all of which are not antithetical to family life but are a natural extension of it.

And what is more, it seems to me that there is a continuity of possibilities of what it means to be human; and those experiences have to do with such emotions as love and guilt, ignorance and confusion regarding vocational goals, loneliness and fear, and the need for affection. Those possible experiences are universal and do not change. The young person ought to receive some sense of the historical continuity of the human species so that his vocational and personal choices might be made intelligently and with sophistication. Bob Dylan ought rightly to be conceived of as a culture hero, but then also should Admiral Perry and Charles Lindbergh and Oliver Wendell Holmes and Booker T. Washington and David Livingston and Savonarola and Copernicus and Moses and George Washington and Crispus Attucks. You really cannot appreciate Bob Dylan without an appreciation of the others on this list of America's culture heroes. To do so is to shortchange oneself in the most brutal of human ways, to conceive of one's own consciousness as an "adequate" indicator of reality, superior to someone else's. But it is a fact that the human condition remains the same and all Americans, even the liberated youth, participate in the same human impoverishment and stand before the same potentialities for human development as do all other men.

2

TRANSCENDENCE AS THE POSSIBILITY OF HISTORICAL ALTERNATIVES —HERBERT MARCUSE

A. EXPOSITION

1. THE CRITICAL THEORY OF SOCIETY

Marcuse wants a more human and rational society. The intellectual tool he uses to conceive of such a society is what he calls "the critical theory of society,"[1] which has as its task to "identify the tendencies that linked the liberal past with its totalitarian abolition." Marcuse goes on to indicate that the abolition of the liberal past was not isolated in totalitarian regimes such as Fascism but has become a reality in many highly developed democracies. The critical theory of society has to exhibit the means by which "bourgeois freedom could become unfreedom" and to point out as well those socio-political elements that opposed such a transformation.

Marcuse believes that a fundamental paradox can be traced in contemporary democratic societies, for it is the democratic society which has brought about the "abolition of thought." The critical theory of society examines those tendencies in culture which have not allowed man to be autonomous, which Marcuse equates with the essential freedom of man, but which lead instead to "the social organization and administration of the mind." It is important to let Marcuse tell it himself. I think the paragraph that follows summarizes much of what Marcuse means by the critical theory of society:

1. Herbert Marcuse, *Negations: Essays in Critical Theory* (Boston: Beacon Press, 1968).

For it was mind, reason, consciousness, "pure" thought that in the traditional culture was supposed to constitute the autonomy of the subject, the essential freedom of man. Here was the sphere of negation, of contradiction to the established order, of protest, of dissociation, of criticism. Protestantism and the bourgeois revolutions proclaimed the freedom of thought and conscience. They were the sanctioned forms of contradiction—often the only ones—and the most precious refuge of hope. Only rarely and in exceptional cases did bourgeois society dare to infringe on this refuge. Soul and mind were (at least officially) considered holy and awesome! Spiritually and mentally, man was supposed to be as autonomous as possible. This was his inner freedom, which was his authentic and essential freedom; the other liberties were taken care of by the economy and by the state. Normally it was not necessary for society to intervene in this sphere; a total coordination and subordination of individuals was not required. The productive forces had not yet reached that stage of development at which the sale of the products of social labor demanded the systematic organization of needs and wants, including intellectual ones. The market regulated for better or worse the operation and output of a labor apparatus not yet dependent upon uninterrupted mass consumption. At a low level of productive forces, bourgeois society did not yet have the means to administer soul and body without discrediting this administration through terroristic violence. Today total administration is necessary, and the means are at hand: mass gratification, market research, industrial psychology, computer mathematics and the so-called science of human relations. These take care of the nonterroristic, democratic, spontaneous-automatic harmonization of individual and socially necessary needs and wants of autonomy and heteronomy. They assure the free election of individuals and policies necessary for this system to continue to exist and grow. The democratic abolition of thought, which the "common man" undergoes automatically and which he himself carries out (in labor and in the use and enjoyment of the apparatus of production and consumption), is brought about in the "higher learning" by those positivistic and positive trends of philosophy, sociology, and psychology that make the established system into an insuperable framework for conceptual thought.[2]

All of the elements of Marcuse's critical theory of contemporary Western society are here: his value conviction about the essential

2. Ibid., pp. xii–xiii.

nature of man; the culture forms which permitted man's autonomy to come into being and which enabled it to flourish politically and socially and economically; the development of an economic environment which regulated man's freedom; the planned administration of a total society in the so-called advanced democracies; the wedding of political, cultural, and economic management with the behavioral sciences; and the absence of recognition on man's part of what has happened to him, that is, that his freedom has been taken away.

The consequence of this lack of freedom is what Marcuse calls one-dimensional man, man who is not aware of the contradictions in reality and nature. The same man has been delivered over to the existing established regimes, which are conservative and antirevolutionary in character. "The last time that freedom, solidarity, and humanity were the goals of a revolutionary struggle was on the battlefields of the Spanish civil war."[3] And Marcuse believes that the only potential revolutionary force today is that of the young student generation, the black minority, and the permanently unemployed. Only among them is there a hope for an end of inhumanity, an inhumanity which is perpetuated by means of the total administration of the productive forces and the satisfaction of needs. "Productivity and prosperity in league with a technology in the service of monopolistic policies seem to immunize advancing industrial society in its established structure."[4]

Marcuse, following Marx, believes that the transformation of society, "the transformation of quantity into quality," can come about only by the leap into a qualitatively different stage in the economic and social development of man. Such a transformation appears possible (as an "explosive tendency") in the final stage of capitalism, when science and technology free man from the "necessary" forms of labor. The technological world, with all of the inhuman aspects of automation and computer science, also allows for the real possibility of man's withdrawing from the apparatus of his labor to become a thinking, knowing, experimenting, and playing being.[5] The "explosive force"

3. Ibid., p. xv.
4. Ibid., p. xvi.
5. Ibid., p. xix.

that Marx envisioned to bring about the transformation of economic forces may appear in our time as (what Marcuse calls) "the social logic of technology." This could lead to new forms of contradiction, which could be capable of expressing the potentialities of a qualitatively different human existence.

However, for Marcuse our society is basically irrational. This fact means that the revolutionary character of critical theory is paralyzed from within. The capacity which society has for a high level of productivity is the same factor which destroys man's capacity to develop his human capabilities. The ability of society to manage the complexities of the inner relationships of business and government means precisely that its effect upon man is one of repression. Repression in our society operates from a position of strength; repression is planned, administered by powerful bureaucratic forces, which know exactly what they are doing. It is technology rather than terror which keeps man in his place in society, and it does so by an administrative efficiency and by a controlled but increasing standard of living.[6] There is implicit within modern technology a totalitarian tendency. "In this society, the productive apparatus tends to become totalitarian to the extent to which it determines not only the socially needed occupations, skills and attitudes, but also individual needs and aspirations."[7] The productive apparatus is thereby capable of destroying the inherent contradictions which exist between the individual and the society, between what Marcuse calls "private" and "public" existence. Social controls are created which are pleasurable to the individual. He willingly relinquishes his basic nature, that is, his essential freedom, to these social controls. For the individual, they mean a higher standard of living, the capacity to consume conspicuously, the ability to respond to the false needs created by advertising. Individuality is repressed, exploitation is disguised, and the dimensions of possible human experience are severely limited.

Marcuse's critical theory of society implies a number of value judgments: one, that human life is worth living, or rather can be and ought

6. Herbert Marcuse, *One Dimensional Man* (London: Sphere Books Ltd., 1964), p. 9.

7. Ibid., p. 13.

to be made worth living (this is an a priori assumption of social theory); and two, that there do exist in society specific possibilities for the amelioration of human life and specific ways to realize these possibilities.[8] Critical theory must validate objectively and empirically these assumptions. Marcuse rejects metaphysics because critical theory must proceed in a rigorously historical way. Critical theory has the capacity to examine society's quantitative and qualitative material and intellectual resources and attempts to ascertain how these may be used to fulfill the objective of "the optional development and satisfaction of individual needs and faculties with a minimum of toil and misery." Critical theory attempts to determine "among the various possible and actual modes of organizing and utilizing the available resources, which ones offer the greatest chance of optimal development."

Marcuse analyzes contemporary Western society and determines that it is irrational; that its citizenry adheres to false consciousnesses; that thought, hope, aspiration have been surrendered; that misery is preserved in the face of unprecedented wealth; that men are committed to false, not real, interests; and that science and technology control nature in order to control socially man's humanity. Man appears in this society as one-dimensional man. Critical theory is confronted with the enormous task of providing "the rationale for transcending this society," to help man see the need to change his way of life, to find his way from a false to a true consciousness. One-dimensional man is both the product of the repressive society and the source of hope for change. Marcuse speaks of the possibility of qualitative change "as the possibility of transcendence." Transcendence is defined as those "tendencies in history and practice which, in a given society, 'overshoot' the established universe of discourse and action towards its historical alternatives, that is, its real possibilities."[9] By the use of the concept of transcendence, Marcuse resolves the problems inherent within the irrational and dehumanized society. Transcendence means the possibility of the amelioration of human life. But Marcuse believes that an advanced industrial society can contain and

8. Ibid., p. 10.
9. Ibid.

control qualitative change. Transcendence exists, therefore, as that possibility that society cannot contain; and there can be historically a disruptive "accident" or "catastrophe" to effect such a change.

2. ONE-DIMENSIONAL MAN IN A REPRESSIVE SOCIETY

Marcuse insists that society organizes the life of its members by a conscious decision to accept certain "historical" alternatives from those which are available to a society. The historical alternatives are socially given and are determined by the material and intellectual inheritance of that society. The vested, dominant interests of the society make the choice. The choice is made wisely because the dominant interests anticipate the modes of transforming society and the ways by which man and nature are utilized. "Once the project has become operative in the basic institutions and relations, it tends to become exclusive and to determine the development of the society as a whole."[10] When the project becomes operative in an advanced technological society such as ours, it determines the entire consciousness of the society, its "intellectual and material culture." Technological control leads to political control.

Freedom of thought, speech, and conscience were in the past critical ideas. They replaced aged social controls based upon class and status. However, once these freedoms are institutionalized, they no longer function in a critical manner; instead, their expression is controlled by the dominant interests of the society. Independent thinking, individuality of behavior, personal autonomy, the expression of political opposition are all prohibited, thereby reducing the possible alternatives (that is, the possibility of transcendence) from historical realization. Nonconformity within a society has no socially redemptive value and is therefore increasingly absent from the society. Modern society, Marcuse argues, is totalitarian whether it is an authoritarian or nonauthoritarian one because it is a "non-terroristic, economic-technical coordination which operates through the manipulation of needs by vital interests."

Human needs condition the mode of operation of social institutions.

10. Ibid., p. 14.

Needs are seen in terms of whether they are desirable and necessary for the prevailing social institution. Needs can therefore be manipulated by the dominant forces in society. Real needs, or true needs, are to be distinguished from false ones, those which are superimposed upon the individual by particular social interests. These false needs lead to human repression which Marcuse believes is the source of man's misery, suffering, and injustice. To satisfy false needs may make the individual happy, but they in effect deny him the ability to recognize how he is being manipulated. What is worse, their satisfaction leads man to a false sense of security, and lulls man to sleep. Marcuse is especially critical of the manufactured needs "to relax, to have fun, to behave and consume in accordance with the advertisements, to love and hate what others love and hate."[11] These manufactured needs are false needs, their satisfaction is false, and the resultant individual is a repressed and demeaned being. His basic humanity has been manipulated by the society whose dominant interest demands repression. Real needs, or vital ones, are nourishment, clothing, and lodging at "the attainable level of culture." The satisfaction of these needs is the prerequisite for the satisfaction of all needs. Their satisfaction assures the continued fulfillment of man's inherent humanity. Liberation for man depends upon the consciousness of servitude and the replacement of false needs by true ones.

Modern society has effectively suffocated those needs which demand liberation while at the same time it has sustained the destructive and repressive elements within an affluent society:

> Here the social controls exact the overwhelming need for the production and consumption of waste; the need for stupefying work where it is no longer a real necessity; the need for modes of relaxation which soothe and prolong this stupefaction; the need for maintaining such deceptive liberties as free competition at administered prices, a free press that censors itself, free choice between brands and gadgets.[12]

Marcuse is arguing that the notion of liberty in our modern industrial societies is an illusory one. The notion of liberty becomes instead a powerful instrument of domination. Not only is the range of choice

11. Ibid., p. 22.
12. Ibid., p. 23.

among options determined by the society, but what can be chosen and what is chosen by the individual is also determined. And what is the most repressive character of our society is that the so-called freedom to choose goods and services maintains social controls over the individual. They contribute to the individual's alienation from his true self. And alienation is the decisive mark of the dehumanized individual; alienation means that the individual can no longer recognize the contrast or conflict between the given and the possible, between his satisfied and unsatisfied needs, between vital and false needs.

Alienation is the common property of vast masses of people, but the so-called equalization of class distinctions, so long a virtue in the American ethos, is simply an indication of the degree to which needs and their satisfactions are controlled by the establishment. There is little equalization of the classes in the United States. Marcuse believes that there is a great deal of social manipulation and control of people's tastes and ambitions. People are satisfied to fulfill false needs. And it is the accomplishment of the dominant interests in society that the masses are effectively conditioned to be subservient. Furthermore, Marcuse is pessimistic about the possibility of man's effecting a change in his alienated situation. The external controls of society destroy the possibility (and spontaneity) of protest. The inner dimension of man's being is effectively silenced. Practically, there is no longer the capacity for the introduction of transcendence. The individual consciousness and the individual unconscious cannot express themselves apart from public opinion and public control. "Mass production and mass distribution claim the *entire* individual." Reason, which is the critical function of negative thinking, submits to the impact of progress. The achievement of progress whittles down ideological differences, the consequence of which is that alienation is swallowed up. The individual no longer possesses the critical apparatus to recognize his alienation. Man's ideological stances are transformed into the ideology of an industrial culture. Ideology, Marcuse says, is the product of an industrial culture. That means simply that the prevailing technological culture imposes an ideology upon the individual which "sells" the prevailing social system as a whole. "The means of mass transportation and communication, the commodities of lodging, food, and clothing, the irresistible output of the entertainment and information industry carry with them prescribed attitudes and habits, certain intellectual and emotional reactions which bind the consumers more or less pleasantly to the producers and, through the latter, to the whole. The products indoctrinate and manipulate; they promote a false consciousness which is immune against its false-hood."[13]

Marcuse's criticism of man in contemporary society is a devastating one. Consumer freedom implies indoctrination. The climb in social status becomes a way of life and becomes in time the "good life," that life which is so much better than it was before. But such a life militates against qualitative change. One-dimensional man results, that man whose ideas and ambitions are determined for him by a source outside of himself, that of the modern industrial state. Transcendent ideas, aspirations, and objectives are rejected or, what is more inauthentic, redefined in terms of the established universe of discourse. They are then given rational support within the established system. And as a consequence man is completely contained, circumscribed by the way of life of the state. His individuality is lost. His freedom is now an illusion.

But there are certain modes of protest which take on a bohemian or existentialist or even, as Marcuse puts it, a spiritual mode. Marcuse believes these are not authentic forms of transcendence, they are no longer contradictory to the status quo; they are rather "the ceremonial part of practical behaviorism, its harmless negation, and are quickly digested by the status quo as part of its healthy diet."[14]

Marcuse argues for his characterization of one-dimensional man by reference to the development of operationalism in the physical sciences and behaviorism in the social sciences. Empirical thought is the common mode by which one conceives of both scientific operations and human behavior. In this way, the difficult problems of philosophy, sociology, psychology are done away with. A positivism results which not only finds metaphysical questions nonsense, but denies as well the "transcending elements of Reason."[15] The scientist

13. Ibid., p. 26.
14. Ibid., p. 28.
15. Ibid., Chapters VII and VIII.

and the philosopher become allied with social processes, with the result that they aid in the creation of one-dimensional man. Society has established that certain kinds of ideas and behavior are harmful to the ongoing and harmonious development of that society. The scientist and the philosopher, by means of intellectual constructions, render the same ideas and behavior as meaningless. Thereby, historical transcendence becomes metaphysical transcendence. No one accepts such a notion any longer. Reason no longer works in the service of the state. Operational and behavioral perspectives become sacrosanct and perform their own intrinsic functions well. They reject as a consequence the possibility of historical transcendence. Scientific and industrial progress, academic and social behaviorism, theoretical and practical reason are all in league with one another. Man is swallowed up by the grand conspiracy of the one-dimensional man.

3. CONCEPTS OF TRANSCENDENCE

Transcendence in Marcuse's thought is related to the attempt to resolve the problems of one-dimensional man within a repressive society. Within his basic Marxist framework, he finds that the fundamental deterrent to the resolution of one-dimensional man lies in modern man's false consciousness: "The slaves must be free for their liberation before they can become free, and that the end must be operative in the means to attain it."[16] Marx's (and Marcuse's) contention is that the liberation of the working class must be the action of the working class itself. Socialism is the result of the first act of the revolution because revolution is already present in the consciousness and action of the workers. According to Marx the "second phase" of development, that movement from a capitalist to a socialist society, is literally constituted in the first phase. But, Marcuse argues, the consciousness of the worker, as the consciousness of the vast masses of people in society, has been manipulated by the vested interests in society. The worker is satisfied with the kinds of objectives society places before him. The negative character of the disenfranchised masses, that proletarian force which would initiate revolution, does

16. Ibid., p. 47.

not appear to have much ability to accept any historical alternatives other than those established by repressive society.

Nevertheless, Marcuse suggests modes of resolution of the dilemmas of one-dimensional man. These resolutions constitute what he means by transcendence.

a. Marcuse allows for an "artistic alienation," that is, an "aesthetic incompatibility" within the technological society as it is today constituted. He sees the artist as someone conversant with a pretechnological society, a world "in which labor was still a fated misfortune; but a world in which man and labor were not yet organized as things and instrumentalities. . . . In the verse and prose of this pretechnological culture is the rhythm of those who wander or ride in carriages, who have the time and the pleasure to think, contemplate, feel and narrate."[17] Marcuse makes the point that this kind of culture is also a posttechnical one, that is, a kind of culture in which there is a free and conscious alienation from the established forms of life. And Marcuse believes that it is the artist who is the witness to the conscious transcendence of the alienated existence which is therefore a mediated alienation.[18] The artist is the bearer of the consciousness of the incompatibility between the authentic humanity of the individual and the repressive character of the developing society.

Marcuse is troubled, however, by the fact that literature and art do not any longer disturb the established society. Society has absorbed or deleted the artistic dimension by "assimilating its antagonistic contents." This new totalitarianism, as Marcuse calls the advanced technological society, allows for a "harmonizing pluralism," in which contradictions "peacefully coexist in indifference."

> The works of alienation are themselves incorporated into this society and circulate as part and parcel of the equipment which adorns and psychoanalyzes the prevailing state of affairs. Thus they become commercials—they sell, comfort, or excite.[19]

One questions whether Marcuse has not reduced artistic alienation to something other than that which actually exists. And I do not mean

17. Ibid., p. 60.
18. Ibid.
19. Ibid., p. 63.

the kind of popular consumption of the meaningless literary trash, of the Jacqueline Susanns, but rather the disruptive voices of a Franz Kafka and a Bertolt Brecht.

Marcuse is impressed with the work of Samuel Beckett and Rolf Hochhuth and believes that they show the real face of our time. He believes too that the "obscene merger of aesthetics and reality" stands in opposition to scientific and empirical reason. Both Beckett's novels and Hochhuth's play *Der Stellvereter* break through the rationalization and realization of man's imagination in our technological society. Such writers are authentic disturbers of the peace; they portray the place of contradiction and ambiguity in human life and offer few happy solutions to life's elemental problems. Brecht, whom Marcuse quotes extensively, made the point that the contemporary world can be represented in the theater only as it is represented as subject to change. But Brecht believed that this could be achieved only when the individual theatergoer was no longer related solely to the events on the stage. Only when there was estrangement from these events could man truly begin to see what was the nature of the things of everyday life, when "the things of everyday life are lifted out of the realm of the self-evident."[20] The estrangement-effect is art's answer to the threat of behavior manipulation. It is art's attempt to retain the negative in the midst of the false harmony imposed upon man by his repressive society. Artistic alienation is a form of what Marcuse calls the "Great Refusal." It is Marcuse's thesis that the great refusal too has succumbed to the grand system, which he calls desublimation, the psychological consequence of a transformation of a higher culture into a popular one. Desublimated sexuality is expressed in, for example, O'Neill's alcoholics and Faulkner's savages and in Williams' *A Streetcar Named Desire* and Nabokov's *Lolita.*[21] Art, "high culture" as Marcuse calls it, offers a glimpse of the transcendence, even if that glimpse is confused and inchoate. But the glimpse is itself the reality, the underlying conflict resident at the heart of the grand system. Art reveals the internal contradiction within society, and no society is so omniscient or omnipotent that it can smother the expression of the

20. Quoted in ibid., p. 65.
21. Ibid., pp. 69 ff.

contradiction. Tragedy and romance, in the profundities of their expression of the human drama, cannot be managed by technology. I am convinced that art is still the medium for opposition and negativity. In spite of the attempt to smother its "subversive" influence, art bespeaks a world filled with freedom.

b. Marcuse speaks about the mutilation of man and nature brought about by the abstractions of linguistic analysis. What he has in mind is the refusal of man to be limited in his experience to the kind of universe of discourse with which linguistic analysis deals. This "experiential breakup" of ordinary discourse functions as a transcendent concept in Marcuse's thought. Banal language, which does not become part of the universe of ordinary discourse, might describe the real empirical world and function to explain our thinking and talking about it:

> Such analyses (of banal language) elucidate because they transcend the immediate concreteness of the human situation and its expression. They transcend it toward the factors that *make* the situation and the behavior of the people who speak (or are silent) in that situation.[22]

Marcuse is suggesting that language (the sentence in Wittgenstein's analysis) might not function "in order as it is," but rather that the opposite may be the case, that the sentence is "as little in order as the world in which this language communicates." Language resists being pushed into the "straightjacket of common usage." Language instead points to a qualitatively different universe. Marcuse insists upon the right to speak in terms which are other than those of common usage. And he insists that language itself breaks through the barriers of the common universe of discourse, to reveal the complexities of possible human experience beyond ordinary discourse. Marcuse is concerned to show the "universal, larger context in which people speak and act and which gives their speech its meaning." He is objecting to the techniques and procedures of linguistic analysis because they do not allow the real empirical world to be exposed. But his criticism of linguistic analysis is not simply an academic criticism. He objects to all intellectual reductionisms which take the complexities of human

22. Ibid., pp. 143–144.

experience and describe them by means of canons of logic or syntactical rules. "The larger context of experience" can never be analyzed or understood in intellectualistic categories:

> This larger context of experience, this real empirical world, today is still that of the gas chambers and concentration camps, or Hiroshima and Nagasaki, of American Cadillacs and German Mercedes, of the Pentagon and the Kremlin, of the nuclear cities and the Chinese communes, of Cuba, of brain-washing and massacres.[23]

Marcuse wants language to be rooted empirically, not in its abstract sense, but in its political sense. Only then does language reveal the critical analytical method which Marcuse insists is fundamental to an understanding of real human nature and which is revelatory of a world in which man is truly free. Language, for Marcuse, has always a hidden dimension of meaning, "the rule of society over its language." Language is always part of a history, and that history can be read in light of the pressures society imposes upon man's speech.

The abstractions of linguistic analysis only conceal the contradictions and illusions which are present in man's real empirical environment. Marcuse wants to bring language back to its proper function, that is to reveal the individual who "experiences (and expresses) only that which is *given* to him, who has only the facts and not the factors, whose behavior is one-dimensional and manipulated."[24] But human language breaks out of the barriers established by a repressive society and exposes the ambiguities of human life and the general sickness of society that destroys man's humanity. Language itself serves the transcendent function of revealing the qualitative difference between the way things are and the way they were meant to be. Language becomes an instrument to make apparent to man the repressive character of the society in which he lives; it becomes itself an agent of a revolutionary consciousness. It reveals in ordinary discourse the alienation of man from his authentic self. Marcuse speaks of "the transcendent language" and rejects any kind of metaphysical or poetical characterization for it. Rather, transcendent language is that language which refuses to be put into separate abstract categories

23. Ibid., p. 146.
24. Ibid., pp. 147–148.

but which pushes forth into the real world revealing the true nature of the human situation.

Language reveals the historical struggle of man with nature and with society. Man himself becomes the subject of language, but not man as an abstraction from the historical struggle. Man's immediate experience becomes the content and form of language because it is revelatory of where man is in his struggle for authentic existence. Marcuse can also speak of the "mystifying" elements in human society, those irrational factors within the whole operation. In spite of the shift in the "locus of mystification," so that a theory of society has nothing to do with the empirical facts of living, for example, in a large impersonal and dehumanizing city, the mystifying factors continue to emerge. And they are the irrational factors which a repressive society attempts to make impotent and which linguistic analysis attempts to purify. Language speaks what society attempts to exclude or conceal. For Marcuse, the real universe of ordinary language is that of the struggle for existence.

Marcuse can also speak of the politicization of philosophy, so that the proper function of philosophy is to point out the nature and character of the repressive society. Philosophical analysis loses then its abstract quality in favor of the therapeutic task of revealing the manipulated and indoctrinated universe and of leading man to a political resolution of the human condition.

c. Marcuse formulates a concept of "the transcendent project," which allows him to speak of the "truth value of different historical projects." What he is getting at is the way by which one develops criteria for selecting one "qualitative historical alternative" from all of those which are available to man. These criteria must refer to the historical realization of specific forms of human existence. The established society itself has a truth value because it has organized man's struggle with nature. But over against the established society there are other historical possibilities, or "projects," as he calls them, and among them those which would change the established one completely. Marcuse develops criteria to evaluate the objective historical truth of the transcendent project, that is, the alternative historical options:

1. The transcendent project must be in accordance with the real possibilities open at the attained level of the material and intellectual culture.

2. The transcendent project, in order to falsify the established totality, must demonstrate its own *higher* rationality in the three-fold sense that

(a) it offers the prospect of preserving and improving the productive achievements of civilization;

(b) it defines the established totality in its very structure, basic tendencies and relations;

(c) its realization offers a greater chance for the pacification of existence, within the framework of institutions which offer a greater chance for the free development of human needs and faculties.[25]

Marcuse then defines his conception of the transcendent project to include criteria which, empirically defined, humanize the struggle for survival. He refers to these criteria in terms of "the pacification of existence."

Transcendence in Marcuse's thought is that which allows for the possibility of historical alternatives which are open to man. But the historical alternatives are found already within the established social institutions. It is the negative, irrational, contradictory character found within the institutions which is the agent of the dissolution of the institution itself. The "internal refutation within society," as Marcuse calls it, leads to the downfall of the system. The historical negation of the established society makes possible the establishment of a new society. Then qualitative historical change can take place.

It is clear now how Marcuse envisages a change in the existing industrial state. Only when the discontented in society become a real force over against society can there be the possibility of change. Marcuse calls this fact "transcendence within the established conditions of thought and action." This is a negative freedom, freedom from the oppression of the established society. But only such transcendence can effect the revolutionary change necessary to break the power of the established order. Transcendence also allows for the "ingression of liberty into historical necessity," that is, the possibility that men can now make their own history and can do so in the context of given historical conditions. Only as social conditions provoke a real dissociation from the established state of affairs can there be a real

25. Ibid., p. 175.

possibility of qualitative historical change. Only as there is a private as well as a political dissociation can there develop an effective opposition, the force of the irrational, which can provoke change.

Marcuse's notion of the transcendent project is strictly empirical and historical. He is dealing with concrete historical alternatives which can effect a new established society, one in which the social conditions for existence are humanized and in which man can live as a human being in his struggle for survival.

d. Marcuse's concept of "the pacification of existence" offers still another conception of transcendence. The pacification of existence means "the development of man's struggle with man and with nature, under conditions where the competing needs, desires, and aspirations are no longer organized by vested interests in domination and scarcity." The concept of "the pacification of existence," as it is used by Marcuse, refers to those empirical criteria which judge historical alternatives in a qualitative way. This concept thereby provides Marcuse with concrete indices for what it means to exist humanely and rationally within a new society. It is an anticipated objective, one which offers the promise of human fulfillment, but one which as yet does not have historical concretion. At its simplest level, it relates to the possibility of ameliorating the human condition, that is, of making it possible for man to live out his life with freedom and with dignity. It means, at a more advanced level, that technological progress would serve in the struggle for the pacification of nature and society toward the promotion of what Marcuse calls "the art of life."

Technology, and science in the service of technology, must therefore develop a political consciousness. Scientific consciousness must become political consciousness, thereby effecting the means by which the empirical criteria for humanity can be attained. Science and technology must free themselves from all of the particular interests that impede the satisfaction of human needs. They must serve to effect the historical alternative and to bring about the desired qualitative change. "Pacified existence" thus becomes the end of science and technology.

Pacification presupposes the mastery of nature, the reduction of misery and suffering, and the termination of the brutalization of man. Marcuse is confident about his transcendent objective:

> All joy and all happiness derive from the ability to transcend Nature
> —a transcendence in which the mastery of Nature is itself subordinated
> to liberation and the pacification of existence. All tranquility, all delight
> is the result of conscious mediation, of autonomy and contradiction.[26]

Concrete illustrations of the human qualities of the pacification of existence are the refusal of all toughness, togetherness, and brutality; disobedience to the tyranny of the majority; a profession of fear and weakness; a disgust for the perpetuation of the repressive society; a commitment to protest; a willingness to compromise, to cover oneself, to cheat the cheaters.[27] What Marcuse is aiming at is the self-determination of each individual, who freely seeks his own human objectives. Self-determination means not being prompted to behave in a particular way because of socially imposed needs. Finally, enslaving contentment is not self-determination.

B. ANALYSIS AND CRITIQUE

1. THE *DRAMATIS PERSONAE* OF REVOLUTION

I have difficulty immediately with the gathering of Marcuse's outsiders and outcasts who somehow are to form the cadres of the revolutionary force which will bring about the radical change in society. They exist outside the democratic process, their lives are intolerable, they are the exploited and the persecuted. They are the poor and the black and the students and the disenfranchised. Their need to end the intolerable conditions under which they live is most real, so much more so than the liberal's, who simply mouths his opposition to the status quo. They are opposed to the system and are not themselves within the system. They refuse to play the game. Marcuse looks to them as the agents of the change he seeks in a repressive society:

> Their opposition hits the system from without and is therefore not
> deflected by the system; it is an elementary force which violates the
> rules of the game and in doing so reveals it as a rigged game. When
> they get together and go out into the streets, without arms, without

26. Ibid., p. 187.
27. Ibid., p. 190.

protection, in order to ask for the most primitive civil rights, they know they face dogs, stones, and bombs, jail, concentration camps, even death. Their force is behind every political demonstration for the victims of law and order. The fact that they start refusing to play the game may be the fact which marks the beginning of the end of a period.[28]

I think Marcuse is much too sanguine in his estimates of the historical possibilities of this kind of revolution. He recognizes that the protests of the discontented and oppressed may not lead to any substantial change in the body politic, but he does look to those who have pledged themselves to the "great refusal" as the agents of some future revolution. But what kind of revolution? Who are the dramatis personae of a revolution? How do the poor and the students and others of the exploited grab political power for themselves from those who already possess it? And what are the means for such a revolution? Is it a political challenge to the established status quo? Or is it a violent and armed revolution? Or is it a nonviolent, peaceful revolution, aimed at a change in man's spiritual and moral nature? How will it take place, and who shall share in the task of reshaping history?

Marcuse does not tell us. And I am not convinced that he has not promised more than he can fulfill. How can the oppressed poor organize themselves into a revolutionary force and threaten the status and stability of the wealthy capitalistic class? How can they gather a sufficient force to become politically visible? And how can they overcome the ideological schisms within their own force? Or even introduce a revolutionary ideology into the lives of the socially impoverished? How can one group of the oppressed unite with another group to begin to make substantive inroads into the political power structure? Marcuse does not tell us. I am afraid that all he offers is a divisive palliative to the oppressed masses. The oppressed form the negative consciousness which challenges the established order. But how are the negative oppressed masses transformed into a revolutionary power? If the consciousness remains in the realm of consciousness, then Marcuse is asking us to conceive of a spiritual revolution and not a political one, a revolution of one's heart and not of one's head. And if this is so, then he is as naive as Charles Reich, who leads politically

28. Ibid., pp. 200–201.

impotent students into the fray, so that they might be wiped out by the powerful political goons.

The question that Marcuse must answer is: How do the oppressed become a revolutionary force? How do they develop into a politically significant force so that they can gather for themselves some of the power of the establishment or overthrow it altogether?

I would conceive of the kind of revolution that Marcuse desires as involving at least the following elements: a common ideology regarding the means and objectives of revolution; cadres of individuals disciplined in revolutionary methods and pledged to give their lives to the cause of radical social change; a union of many groups of the oppressed, the poor, students, blacks, and urban ghetto dwellers. Marcuse has some kind of Marxist notion of the inevitability of revolution. But no revolution will take place without an organized attempt to grab power from the powerful. Groups of malcontents on the periphery of political power will remain there until they decide to effect some sort of organized protest. The form and extent of the protest is the content of revolution.

2. MARCUSE'S MONOLITHIC POLITICAL ANALYSIS

Closely allied with this first criticism is Marcuse's inability to look at the body politic in pluralistic terms. To abandon the democratic process as a means to effect social change is one thing; not to recognize that the political totality in the United States is made up of a multiplicity of forces and factors is quite another. To categorize all political activity in the United States as part of a grand conspiracy to maintain the repressive society is a simplistic analysis of what is actually going on. To believe that most of it is harmless activity, channeled through institutionalized democracy, including the so-called democratic liberals' efforts, may be an accurate estimation of the present situation in the United States. But not all of it can be characterized in so simplistic a manner. There are authentic revolutionaries *within* the democratic system, and not all of them are misguided idealists who have not recognized the manipulation of their consciousnesses by the bureaucrats and the military generals. The conspiracy against freedom is insidious, but it is not omnipresent. The military-industrial complex is capable of controlling human experience, but it is not omnipotent. Freedom has the remarkable capacity to emerge from the shattering challenge to its uniqueness and to continue to live and to protest and to blossom into new forms of personal and social experience.

Marcuse and his revolutionary manifesto are expressions of the inability of the technological society to control completely the desire on the part of man to be free. Marcuse recognizes "artistic alienation" as a form of the opposition to the repressive society. And ordinary language itself, he argues, can never be reduced merely to analytical formulas. Language expresses the hard-won humanity of man and can never be stilled.

What I am suggesting is that Marcuse's notion of transcendence is a functional corrective to the dehumanization of the one-dimensional society. Marcuse may exaggerate somewhat the ability of modern society to control man; but he errs completely when he finds little hope for man within that society. Marcuse is deluded if he believes that there is no hope for modern society *or* that modern society can contain the negative and irrational forces within it. That it cannot do. Man has the remarkable capacity to refuse to be subjected to totalitarianisms of all kinds, even the most recent one that Marcuse has described so powerfully.

I have argued that consciousness must be translated into political terms. But man as a free being, created with a capacity for a free expression of his humanity, can never be completely won over to a manipulative system. Man's freedom will always emerge from the managed society, and it will always threaten the autonomy and stability of that society. But it must challenge the status quo in aggressive *political* ways. Marcuse hardly ever demonstrates how that is possible without destroying the political system entirely. But he nowhere demonstrates how the political system will be destroyed. Certainly it cannot be destroyed by politically impotent, politically insensitive, socially disenchanted types, whose "consciousness" alone will change the system. What Marcuse suggests is some sort of transcendental power manipulating the system to lead the disenchanted revolution. But such a notion is politically naive and, what is more, dangerous to the objectives of those revolutionaries who are conscious of the power resident within political systems. What I am proposing is similar to what Marcuse is proposing, that is, the radical termination of the repressive society. But I want the change to come about in classic revolutionary ways, by the deliberate attempt of the repressed minorities to obtain for themselves political power. Only when they have achieved some kind of popular political base can they begin to manipulate that power to effect rational and humanistic objectives.

Marcuse's conception of political involvement is useful at this point.[29] He uses a study by Julian L. Woodward and Elmo Roper, "Political Activity of American Citizens," as illustrative of the kind of possible political activity in the United States. Woodward and Roper use an "operational" definition of the term political activity, which means essentially how Americans behave politically: voting at the polls, supporting possible pressure groups, personally communicating directly with legislators, participating in political party activity, engaging in habitual dissemination of political opinions through word-of-mouth communication. Marcuse is convinced that these five forms of political behavior cannot serve to separate those people who are active in national political issues from those who are not; they do not allow the individual to recognize the "technical and economic contacts between corporate business and the government, and among the key corporations themselves." Furthermore, they do not permit any authentic discrimination between the real political issues and the issues which the publicity media decide are significant; and they certainly do not allow for unpopular political points of view to be expressed and to be counted in the political arena.

But Marcuse is wrong. There is a deficiency in the modes of political expression in the United States, but that expression does not, and cannot, preclude the expression of a minority and opposing point of view. I cannot conceive of any sacrosanct political machine which allows for all forms of ideological expression, but I have seen examples of the disenfranchised and the politically invisible (the Southern blacks, the California Mexican-Americans) becoming part of the American political power configuration. And they too have become so *not* in some magical way, waiting for the appropriate spiritual revolution. Rather they have forced their way into the hallowed halls

29. Ibid., pp. 101 ff.

of Congress and have political power for themselves. Legislation has, as a consequence, been enacted which begins to reveal more of the true picture of the American body politic. Such change comes about not by the consciousness of the socially disenchanted but rather by the aggressive confrontation in the streets of the established power structures. Revolutions entail the transference of political power: the have-nots become included among the haves. And no other kind of revolution is a real one within the American political arena.

Marcuse has abandoned the democratic ways of effecting social change but offers no alternatives (except the spiritual ones). There is no place to go; and the result can only be absolute dejection and frustration.

Marcuse also speaks about political freedom as "liberation of the individuals from politics over which they have no effective control." But what then is the sphere of politics over which they can have some control? Again, liberation comes not from the abandonment of power but from the realization of power. Real revolution is always effected by political agents, who bring about a radical reorientation of the political structures in American society.

3. MARCUSE'S ANTIMETAPHYSICAL STANCE

Marcuse's discussion of the relationship between science and metaphysics presents a number of valued problems. Marcuse speaks about the functionality of scientific abstractions, that is, that they can be used to promote the physical qualities of the good life. They serve to transform the established universe into a new one. But philosophical abstractions are disfunctional because they have not served to conquer and transform nature. "The final philosophic concepts remained indeed metaphysical; they were not and could not be verified in terms of the established universe of discourse and action."[30]

Metaphysical propositions, therefore, Marcuse argues, tend to become physical and historical. Or borrowing an analogy from Saint-Simon, the metaphysical stage of civilization has come to an end, and it is the scientific which now dominates modern society. Scientific

30. Ibid., p. 181.

"rationality," as Marcuse calls it, is translated into political power in the higher industrial societies. The question is then posed, "Does political power lead to the promotion of the 'art of life'?" Marcuse thinks it can and believes that scientific "rationality" can "project and definite (sic) the possible realities of a free and pacified existence." Science or reason, "the scientific reason," could elaborate the nature of the qualitatively new life offered by technology. Marcuse writes:

> Within the established societies, the continued application of scientific rationality would have reached a terminal point with the mechanization of all socially necessary but individually repressive labour. . . . But this stage would also be the end and limit of the scientific rationality in its established structure and direction. Further progress would mean the *break,* the turn of quantity into quality. It would open the possibility of an essentially new human reality—namely, existence in free time on the basis of fulfilled vital needs. Under such conditions, the scientific project itself would be free for trans-utilitarian ends, and free for the "art of living" beyond the necessities and luxuries of domination. In other words, the completion of the technological reality would be not only the prerequisite, but also the rationale for *transcending* the technological reality.[31]

But Marcuse has described his technological revolution in such a way that there emerges from the same scientific environment (which created the one-dimensional man) the transcendent force which brings about a new humanized society. But he cannot have it both ways; either the scientific-technological society demeans and dehumanizes man, or it effects a truly human environment. If it does both, as Marcuse maintains, then there must be introduced the factor of values in the break from quantitative concerns into qualitative ones. Or does Marcuse believe in some omniscient power, a transcendent power that oversees the move from a dehumanized society to a human one? If he does so, then he is subject to those criticisms that are made of Marxists, that there is hidden within the historical dialectic a virulent metaphysics, a notion of economic "providence," a kind of secularized *heilsgeschichte,* which moves magically and trans-historically upon the course of historical events.

31. Ibid., p. 182.

Marcuse expressly denies that he wants to revive "values."[32] The scientific and technological transformation of man and nature is autonomous unto itself; it does not need spiritual or any other kind of values. Technology and science have rendered possible "the translation of values into technical tasks—the materialization of values." But what can this translation mean in terms of the definition of what it means to be human? Surely, humanity must be defined in concrete and realistic terms, so that it is the real man we are concerned with and not some abstract concept of man. But unless there is a definition of man which offers characteristics of humanity which go beyond the technological definition, then man cannot emerge from the one-dimensional sphere in which technology has placed him. If he is human or if science and technology will help him to be human, then science and technology cannot define what that humanity entails. Another conception is necessary; and that conception can only come from a realization of certain unique and inalienable values that human beings possess and which they do not possess in a one-dimensional society.

What is required is a conception of humanity and of freedom which can be translated into specific empirical indices of humanity and freedom. For example, one can speak of freedom in terms of vocational choices, political and civil rights, the availability of public housing, free schools, cultural and recreational opportunities, and so forth. But that conception of freedom transcends the conception of freedom which science and technology, even in their most advanced forms, offer. It seems to me that it is only possible to deal politically with science and technology when science and technology are given specific moral objectives which must be fulfilled historically.

4. REASON AS A TRANSCENDENT CONCEPT

Marcuse's concept of reason functions as a transcendent concept. It must be reason, or scientific rationality, which gives to the historical alternative its moral character and which effects the transformation from quantity to quality. Reason then is both the force behind the

32. Ibid.

historical change and the characteristic of the kind of humanized society that Marcuse envisages.

Marcuse believes that the one-dimensional society has transformed the rational into the irrational; what is actually irrational has been made to appear to be rational. He writes: "The advancing one-dimensional society alters the relation between the rational and the irrational. Contrasted with the fantastic and insane aspects of its rationality, the realm of the irrational becomes the home of the really rational—of the ideas which may promote 'the art of life.' "[33] Marcuse believes, and rightly so, that the contradictory and negative elements of life burst through the social façade that the one-dimensional society creates. What this means is that there is always a challenge to the status quo and it comes from the strangest of places, from the protesting youth, from the artistically alienated, and from the socially and economically depressed. The life of the one-dimensional society is therefore never secure because negation persists within its structures and threatens its ultimate survival. What I question in Marcuse's analysis of the irrational-rational continuum is whether the rational ought to be conceived of as the normative human category. "What is rational has been made to appear irrational." But can one make such a claim if the very stuff of reality, the essence of humanity, is not itself rational, but irrational? That is, if man's authentic nature is the opposition to the one-dimensional mold and if authentic human nature is characterized by the negative and contradictory character of life, why assign the category of reason to it? Reason must share in the same contradictions and irrationalities of human existence and cannot then properly be called rational. Man's nature and the environment for the growth and development of that nature is filled with ambiguity and confusion. There is no transcendent category which will elevate man above his authentic nature and above the absurdities of life, least of all reason, which participates fully in those absurdities. Marcuse presents a critical theory of society which painstakingly locates the negative character within our society, which alters the development and subsequent shape of that society. But to conceive of a "rational" goal of society, a society which successfully effects a final and

33. Ibid., p. 194.

ultimate historical change from quantity to quality, because of an intrinsic rationality or scientific rationality is a monstrous illusion. Marcuse can then only offer another version of those impossible utopias that realistic thinkers have long ago rejected as historically irrelevant.

Marcuse ultimately is faced with an alternative: society comes into being because of the revolutionary forces of opposition within the established society, or the industrialized society is so complete in its domination of man that it is wholly capable of containing those forces of opposition. But change will never come about because of the "historic pull" of reason. Reason, too, is perverse and has been manipulated by the power-brokers, who want the opposition to believe all over again in illusory chimeras, or utopian societies, that can never be historically realized.

5. MARCUSE'S LANGUAGE GENERALIZATIONS

Fundamental to any critical evaluation of Marcuse must be an appraisal of the general terms he uses: society, democracy, industrialized society, and so forth. It is difficult not to recognize the pluralistic character of these terms. For example, when Marcuse speaks of the control society has over one's imagination, he says: "In reducing and even cancelling the romantic space of imagination, society has forced the imagination to prove itself on new grounds, on which the images are translated into historical capabilities and projects."[34] What then of those expressions of imagination that society has not been able to control? And what about the imaginative character of society itself, which we might conceive of as those developments in society that tend to humanize rather than to brutalize life. The problem with Marcuse is that he looks at society as he does history, in a monolithic way, and allows for no historical exceptions. The good guys are always good, and the bad guys are always bad, and they are always against one another. In the case of Marcuse, it is a whole host of bad guys organized together to crush any attempt on the part of the good guys to effect any change in society.

34. Ibid., p. 195.

But history does not permit such a simplistic reading. The people never effect revolution, as society never functions as a totalitarian force. Some people, with a common ideology and a common sense of historical destiny, effect revolutions. Society has those factors within it—the military-industrial complex, the arrogant powermongers, the warlords—who act to hold man down and destroy his humanity. The enemy must be labeled if it is to be challenged. And there is an enemy, and it is powerful and seeks for more power and will not cease until it controls all of society. But that enemy must be located if it is to be combatted. The lines must be drawn in order to wage war. Unless we do that, we go flaying about with much sound and fury but little visible alternatives to the concrete historical process.

Marcuse's notion of transcendence as the possibility of historical alternatives is a functional one *only* when man, that is, specific historical man, is permitted to act upon the stage of history, consciously and deliberately, with the intention to alter the course of that history. Unless Marcuse allows for that possibility, then his conception of revolution is as utopian as his conception of society is monolithic. What I am arguing for is man's freedom to determine his own destiny. But to permit such an objective to be real, man must become a historical actor, who intends by and for himself to alter historical events. But then it is not "society" he objects to, but those concrete social expressions of totalitarianism within his society that he intends to uproot. That is a task which becomes a political one, to manipulate and destroy when it is strategic to do so those instruments of political power which destroy man's freedom. It is unrealistic to think of the inevitability of revolution, and it is not constructive to believe in the ubiquity of evil. Marcuse's simplistic notions of good and evil and society and the revolution do not do justice to concrete historical realities. They obfuscate the issues and do not provoke oppressed men to do battle against the oppressors.

3

TRANSCENDENCE
AS *CREATIO EX NIHILO*
—R. D. LAING

A. EXPOSITION

Laing wants to turn us on, all of us; he wants to drive us out of our wretched minds! That really is not a bad generalization about the intention of Laing's psychotherapeutic method. In a variety of works, some of which are clinical and academic studies—for example, *Interpersonal Perception; Sanity, Madness and the Family; The Divided Self* —and others, of an emotive and mystical character—*The Politics of Experience, The Bird of Paradise,* and *Knots*—Laing wants to reorient our self-consciousness and make us become aware of ourselves and others and nature and society and the world we live in, in radically new ways. And Laing has worked quite sensitively with the concept of transcendence as he has tried to bring about a change in human awareness. While treating schizophrenic patients, Laing discovered that extreme ego loss could be analyzed in ways similar to the experiences described by mystics throughout the centuries. Common to the experience of many of his patients was an experience filled with mystical and religious imagery. He found that often psychotic breaks were directed by a "will towards health" and, when allowed to run a natural course, led to a positive reintegration of the self. The patient gained great personal insight and improved social integration. It was an experience similar to a spiritual awareness of the "totality of all things." Laing called his treatment of psychoses "voyages of discovery." His patients emerged from their psychoses with deeper and broader personalities and with a greater understanding of themselves and the world in which they lived.

Transcendence becomes a basic category in Laing's psychotherapeutic methodology. By transcendence he means the process of becoming whole, or the restoration of ego health, of the ecstatic experience of the soul's unity with God, or of mystic illumination. Whatever Laing means precisely by transcendence is not so important: it is that ineffable, unbelievable, more-than-empirical experience that puts all of life back together again. Therefore, when reading Laing and attempting to understand his psychoanalytic method, it might be that we are treading on ground that does not reveal the mystery of his analytical system. And that might be Laing's underlying assumption; that is, that the experience that gives wholeness is not itself subject to analysis and criticism. As it is impossible to put the mystic's moment of unity into cognitive terms or ordinary language, so it is impossible to describe the "discovery" of the schizophrenic that reintroduces him to reality.

Laing, however, offers significant aids for the contemporary quest for ego health, and these might be considered as an extraordinary breakthrough in modern psychoanalytic theory. And in a unique way, his insights about the self are representative of what Jewish and Christian theologians have meant by transcendence.

1. PERSONALISTIC INTERPRETATION OF MAN-IN-COMMUNITY

Laing intends nothing less than "a thoroughly self-conscious and self-critical human account of man." Such an account is necessary, Laing believes, because of the basic estrangement of human life, the alienation of every man from his authentic self. But this realization is the occasion for the serious attempt to reconstruct man's inner life. The fact of human alienation is given:

> We are bemused and crazed creatures, strangers to our true selves, to one another, and to the spiritual and material world—man, even from an ideal standpoint, we can glimpse but not adopt. We are born into a world where alienation awaits us. We are potentially men, but are in an alienated state, and this state is not simply a natural system. Aliena-

tion as our present destiny is achieved only by outrageous violence perpetrated by human beings on human beings.[1]

Laing attempts then to reconstruct the human state, so that man can be authentically human. His task is not alien to that of Marx, Kierkegaard, Freud, Tillich, and others, whose allegiance he is readily willing to acknowledge.

Laing rejects behavioristic notions of psychology and psychotherapy; these disciplines have to do with a person's experience, and that experience is always a unique one. "The other person's behavior is an experience of mine. My behavior is an experience of the other. The task of social phenomenology is to relate my experience of the other's behavior to the other's experience of my behavior."[2] Psychology and psychotherapy deal with the "inter-experience" of human beings. However, methodological concerns remain. One can observe another person's behavior, but cannot see the experience one person has of another. Furthermore, the experience I have of another person is not in any way "inside" me. I experience a person as that person simply is. But as my experience of another person is invisible to me, so that experience is also invisible to the other person. One's experience is not another's. One cannot know another person's experience. Men are invisible to one another.

Yet it is experience which provides the only evidence that a man has of his relationship to another human being. There is a distinction between experiencing one's experience and the experience of one as experiencing. That for Laing is the decisive difference between behavioristic and what I suppose he might call experiential techniques of psychotherapy:

> The study of the experience of others is based on inferences I make, from my experience of you experiencing me, about how you are experiencing me experiencing you experiencing me. . . .[3]

The continuity Laing describes is that of the continuity of human experience. Psychology and psychotherapy are scientific disciplines of one's own and of others' experiences. These disciplines concern them-

1. R. D. Laing, *The Politics of Experience* (Middlesex, Great Britain: Penguin Books, 1967), pp. 11 ff.
2. Ibid., p. 15.
3. Ibid., p. 16.

selves with the science of *inter-experience.* Its concern for behavior is as I experience it. Inferences are made on the basis of experience: "I seek to make evident to the others, through their experience of my behavior, what I infer of your experience, through my experience of your behavior."[4]

Laing proceeds to argue that the relationship between experience and behavior is not the province of the natural scientist. The relationship is not one which can be dealt with in an objective way, so that certain kinds of experiences are treated as authentic problems and others are not. What he has in mind is the classic scientific disaffection for so-called "inner" subjective experiences. He rejects this popular scientific prejudice in order to allow some traditional nonscientific concepts, such as soul, psyche, imagination, fantasy, reverie, and dreams, to be discussed by the psychotherapist. Laing cannot justify the age-old distinction that assigns such phenomena to the "inner" side of man, which is over against the outer. These phenomena are simply different forms of experience; they serve to allow man to experience the further reaches of his being. This distinction is crucial to Laing's subsequent discussion of transcendence.

Laing defines a person "in terms of experience, as a center of orientation of the objective universe; and in terms of behavior, as the origin of actions."[5] But persons are not objects to be studied; they are beings who are capable of experience. Experience becomes the focal point for Laing's discussion of the person. The person is you or me, that being through whom objects are experienced. However, the person does not exist in isolation from other persons. His world is composed of relationships with others: a social field of reciprocal influence and interaction. Laing describes the person in this way: "I experience myself, identifiable as Ronald Laing by myself and others, as experienced by me and acted upon by others, who refer to that person I call 'me' as 'you' or 'him,' or grouped together as 'one of us' or 'one of them' or 'one of you.' "[6] The objectivity of personal relations are thereby established by this experiential method. The proper study of the person, Laing insists, includes more than the sum of the in-

4. Ibid., p. 17.
5. Ibid., p. 20.
6. Ibid., p. 21.

dividual's behavioral parts. Observation about behavior must lead to inferences about individual experience. Only then does one deal authentically with that which we call the human species.

Up to this point Laing has argued that (1) behavior is always a function of experience; (2) experience and behavior are always related to someone or something other than the individual self. This relationship Laing calls "the dialogic character of human experience, when two (or more) persons are in relation, the behavior of each towards the other is mediated by the experience by each of the other, and the experience of each is mediated by the behavior of each."[7] Experience directs itself irresistibly to the experience of another.

The so-called normal individual is a poor example of what a human person can be. Laing insists that contemporary man is in bad shape: man has lost his capacity to think; his common sense is deluded; he cannot see, hear, touch, taste, or smell in a real way; his "inner world" is lost; realms of experience remain foreign to him; his imagination is gone; even the use of his body is perverse.

> What we call "normal" is a product of repression, denial, splitting, projection, introjection and other forms of destructive action on experience. It is radically estranged from the structure of being.[8]

The so-called normal man is the alienated man. He is asleep, unconscious, and out of his mind. Society educates the normal man to be absurd, and thus he is normal. Laing reminds his reader that normal man has killed perhaps 100 million of his fellow normal human beings over the last ten years. And the reason for such barbaric behavior is simply that man's experience has been destroyed. Because it has been destroyed, man's behavior becomes destructive. Man's humanity is thereby lost. And man is capable of destroying the humanity of other men. The reason for such a possibility is the given interdependent character of human existence. "We are both acted upon," Laing writes, "changed for good or ill, by other men; and we are agents who act upon others to affect them in different ways. Each of us is the other to the other."[9] This, in essence, is Laing's interpretation of the person-in-community. But the mood of his analysis of the human condition

7. Ibid., p. 22.
8. Ibid., pp. 23–24.
9. Ibid., pp. 25–26.

is a pessimistic one. Man is in danger of self-annihilation. And the most antihumanistic aspect of such an act is that a man is capable of destroying vast segments of the population along with himself. But Laing announces that he is an optimist about the future, for every child born is "a new spark of life," a potentially new being who can bring new light and life into the world. There is a decidedly evangelical character to Laing's language at this point. Indeed, there seems to be a basic religious character to his psychotherapeutic methodology.

Laing searches for ways to provide meaning for human existence. He suggests that the first way that the world has made sense to man continues to provide a framework or superstructure for subsequent experiences. However, for most people, the first way by which the world has become meaningful has been the experience of fantasy. Fantasy need not be an irrational and immature experience; it can be a meaningful and mature way of relating to one's world. Fantasy may be an essential ingredient of our unconsciousness, but we may also give a "fantastic" meaning to our actions. Fantasy may be the experiential and relational side of human behavior. In that sense, fantasy is not irrelevant to man's makeup, but rather it is an essential ingredient in all of his behavior. Fantasy, for Laing, is always experiential and meaningful, and when man is associated affirmatively with his fantasy, it becomes relational in a real sense. Laing provides this illustration of the phenomenon of fantasy:

> Peter is trying to get through to Paul. He feels that Paul is being needlessly closed up against him. It becomes increasingly important to soften or get to Paul. But Paul seems hard, impervious, and cold. Peter feels he is beating his head against a brick wall. He feels tired, hopeless, progressively more empty as he sees he is failing. Finally he gives up. Paul feels, on the other hand, that Peter is pressing too hard. He feels he has to fight him off. He doesn't understand what Peter is saying, but feels he has to defend himself from an assault.[10]

The point Laing is making in this illustration is that both Peter and Paul are dissociated from their own fantasy and from the fantasies of the other, with the consequence that there is no real relationship between them.

10. Ibid., pp. 27–28.

The alternative is a true human relationship, in which the behavior of one person is experienced by another in a special way. "How she behaves towards him influences how he experiences her. And his experience of her contributes to his way of behaving towards her, etc. . . ."[11] Experience becomes the focal point for all human relationships. Those relationships can be enriching or demeaning, creative or destructive. A person can affirm another person's being or he can deny it. And he can do so in the context of the normal alienation of one man from another, which in itself is destructive of one's experience and that of another.

The process of "dealienation" involves the individual's realization of himself and of the many different modes of the expression of the alienation. These are the so-called defense mechanisms with which the professional psychotherapist must deal. Laing makes the point that the expression of one man's alienation from another man is not unconscious but is found in the deliberate and conscious ways by which he perpetuates the alienation. Laing wants to bring the patient back into the realm of responsibility, so that he becomes aware of what he is doing; so that the patient becomes an agent of reconciliation. The defense mechanism is an action taken by the person which is derived from his own experience. He then dissociates himself from his action. The consequence of such behavior is that the person no longer experiences himself as a person. He feels himself as a part of a person. Strange disruptive mechanisms are at work within him; it is these with which the psychotherapist must deal. But Laing insists that such a procedure of dealing with a person is all wrong. The defenses are personal actions upon oneself and upon others. They are actions which are based upon experience.

People are capable of what Laing calls "transpersonal invalidation"; that is, a person may relate to another person in such a way as to make him feel that his experience is meaningless and may make him feel guilty about it to boot! To make the invalidation really effective, Laing suggests that one overlay it with a thick patina of mystification. One can then deny that one is attempting to invalidate another's experience. One can suggest that he is paranoid, for example.[12]

11. Ibid., p. 29.
12. Ibid., pp. 30 ff.

What then is the resolution to man's alienation, his alienation from himself and from another? Laing relates his answer to the notion of man's involving himself in the continual process of creation, of enabling being to emerge from nonbeing. One man becomes the creator of another being in the sense that a relationship is established between himself and another individual. Laing's interpretation of man-in-community is thereby a dynamic one. Man causes another being to come into being by entering into an active and creative relationship. Laing puts it this way:

> The ground of the being of all beings is the relation between them. This relationship is the 'is,' the being of all things, and the being of all things is itself no-thing. Man creates in transcending himself in revealing himself.
> ... The experience of being the actual medium for a continual process of creation takes one past all depression or persecution or vainglory, past even chaos or emptiness, into the very mystery of the continual flip of nonbeing into being, and can be the occasion of that great liberation when one makes the transition from being afraid of nothing, to the realization that there is nothing to fear.[13]

Laing can then make the extraordinary statement that one's stance in relation to the process of creating being from nonbeing is decisive as to whether one is mad or sane! And Laing is careful to describe the act of creation as possible with all human relationships. Little benefit is derived from the concentration of creativity upon oneself. Creation from nonbeing to being is always the creation of another human being-in-relationship. This then is the miracle that Laing encourages his readers to envisage:

> From the point of view of a man alienated from his source creation arises from despair and ends in failure. But such a man has not trodden the path to the end of time, the end of space, the end of darkness, and the end of light. He does not know that where it all ends, there it all begins.[14]

13. Ibid., p. 36.
14. Ibid., p. 38.

2. ONTOLOGICAL SECURITY AND SCHIZOPHRENIA

A man who has a sense of himself as a real, live, and whole person with a sense of history ("in a temporal sense, a continuous person") is what Laing calls an ontologically secure person. His existence is secure. He meets the usual hazards of life with a sense of his own identity, but even more, with a sense of the identity of others. When these senses are lacking, the person is insecure.

> The individual then may experience his own being as real, alive, whole; as differentiated from the rest of the world in ordinary circumstances so clearly that his identity and autonomy are never in question; as a continuum in time; as having an inner consistency, substantiality, genuineness and worth; as spatially coextensive with the body; and usually as having begun in or around birth and liable to extinction with death. He thus has a firm core of ontological security.[15]

Others have no sense of ontological security. The individual may feel that he is more unreal than real. He may constantly question his place in the world. He may lack a sense of consistency and cohesiveness. He may feel that he is made up of an incorporeal body; or he may question the value and validity of his body. His relationship to others is fragmented and insecure. He feels threatened by forces and powers "out there." He is the ontologically insecure person. The ordinary circumstances of life challenge his feeble sense of security.[16]

Laing has devised a new and original way to conceive of the schizophrenic experience. The person's so-called sanity or mental health is measured along a continuum, the poles of which are primary ontological security and primary ontological insecurity. Laing argues that the ontological subject (or existential subject) must come to terms with a fundamental human issue, that is, to acknowledge the existence of the self in the face of the contradictions and threats to its survival. When a position of ontological security has been reached, the ordinary circumstances of life do not overwhelm the assurance that the

15. R. D. Laing, *The Divided Self, An Existential Study in Sanity and Madness* (London: Tavistock Publications, 1960), pp. 41–42.

16. *The Divided Self* is replete with examples of the ontologically insecure person; cf. especially Part II.

self has of its own stability and continuance. When such a position has not been reached, then the daily everyday circumstances will pose a devastating threat. Such a person senses that he lives in a "world of his own." He will try all kinds of ways to try to remain "real," to keep alive, to preserve his identity. External events do not affect him in the same way as they might another, and often his world is not a world that he is capable of sharing with other people. The term "schizoid" is used for that personality whose experiences are split in two ways: first, there is a split in his relationship to the world; and second, there is a disruption in his relationship to himself. Laing's clinical definition of the schizoid is this: "Such a person is not able to experience himself 'together' with others or 'at home in the world,' but on the contrary, he experiences himself in despairing aloneness and isolation; moreover, he does not experience himself as a complete person but rather as 'split' in various ways, perhaps as a mind more or less tenuously linked to a body, as two or more selves, and so on."[17]

Laing does attempt theoretically and clinically to discover the genesis of the ontologically insecure person. He calls his approach "existential-phenomenological," which he defines as the attempt "to set all particular experiences within the context of his whole being-in-his-world." By means of this approach, he hopes to understand the existential context of the schizophrenic, the schizophrenic qua person, and to describe what he calls "a comprehensive transition" from the sane schizoid way of being-in-the-world to the psychotic way of being-in-the-world.

Laing is impressed with Erving Goffman's analysis of mental patients.[18] Goffman discovered that to see the so-called mentally disturbed patient in the context in which his behavior takes place sheds more light on the genesis of schizophrenia than the classic psychoanalytic categories, for example, what might be called "intrapsychic regression." Laing in his own clinical studies verified Goffman's findings.[19] He calls the schizophrenic experience without exception "a

---

17. Ibid., p. 17.
18. Erving Goffman, *Essays on the Social Situation of Mental Patients and Other Inmates* (Garden City, N.Y.: Doubleday-Anchor Books, 1961).
19. R. D. Laing and A. Esterson, *Sanity, Madness and the Family* (London: Tavistock Publications, 1964).

special strategy that a person invents in order to live in an unlivable situation."[20] The observation of Gregory Bateson makes the same point and is well worth quoting:

> It would appear that once precipitated into psychosis the patient has a course to run. He is, as it were, embarked upon a voyage of discovery, which is only completed by his return to the normal world, to which he comes back with insights different from those of the inhabitants who never embarked on such a voyage.[21]

Schizophrenia becomes for Laing a functional category, in that the label schizophrenia does not refer to a "condition" but to a social fact or, as Laing would have it, a political event. What that means is that the individual is labeled as psychologically maladaptive and therefore pathological by his society. But Laing insists that social and psychological adaption to a dysfunctional society might be of greater danger to the individual and to the society than maladaptation. He illustrates this point by reference to the perfectly adjusted bomber pilot, who he believes may be a greater threat to the survival of the human species than the hospitalized schizophrenic who is convinced that the bomb is inside himself. Laing argues that schizophrenic behavior may therefore be a satisfactory form of alienation from the alienated society within which man lives.

When a person is labeled as a schizophrenic he enters a "political" realm, that is, he fulfills a role which is determined for him by the society in which he lives. He is a patient, a mentally sick man; he no longer is "in control of himself"; he is not allowed to have a definition for his self; he is no longer treated as a human agent or a responsible person. He is invalidated as a human being, without minimal civil rights. He is controlled by his society. And thus his social maladaptation has become a political event.

The understanding of schizophrenia suggests the proper treatment. Understanding the person appears to be the sine qua non of Laing's psychotherapeutic method. "The art of understanding those aspects of an individual's being which we can observe, as expressive of his

20. Laing, *The Politics of Experience*, p. 95.
21. G. Bateson, ed., *Perceval's Narrative: A Patient's Account of His Psychosis* (Stanford: Stanford Univ. Press, 1961), pp. xiii–xiv; quoted from Laing, ibid., pp. 97–98.

mode of being-in-the-world, requires us to relate his actions to his way of experiencing the situation he is in with us."[22] Understanding the person means a number of other things: first, that we understand the individual in terms of his present. This is the way to understand his past. Second, it means that we assign no predetermined labels to the individual's behavior, such as to suggest that he is suffering from a "disease." The psychotic individual is first of all a human person and ought to be treated as such. For Laing's existential phenomenological approach to the psychotherapeutic method, this means at least that the personalities of the doctor and the patient do not ipso facto stand in opposition to one another. Rather, the doctor may have to enter the peculiar world of the psychotic. "He draws on his own psychotic possibilities without foregoing his sanity."[23]

Laing believes that it is necessary for the doctor to know intimately what the patient is experiencing, including his experience of the doctor. And the knowledge of the patient is not an intellectual one but a profoundly experiential one. In this connection, Laing uses the term love. The love of the patient, who is also the neighbor, is never the love for an abstract clinical case or a textbook schizophrenic. The patient is schizophrenic, but he must be known and not manipulated. He cannot be treated as if he had "gotten" a disease known as schizophrenia. He must be loved for the person he is. That knowledge, that acceptance, must be communicated to the individual. The doctor-patient relationship takes on what Christians call an agapeic relationship. Laing wants the doctor to love his schizophrenic patient, and he is certain that only in such a relationship can health be restored. Laing describes the relationship between doctor and patient in these extraordinary words:

> The therapist's hate as well as his love is, therefore, in the highest degree relevant. What the schizophrenic is to us determines very considerably what we are to him, and hence his actions.[24]

Ontological security is largely dependent upon another's relationship to me. That is to say, with the sane person there is the expectation

22. Laing, *The Divided Self,* p. 32.
23. Ibid., p. 34.
24. Ibid.

that my conception of myself will be shared, and endorsed, by another person. When two sane people meet, there is a reciprocal relation of each other's identities. There are several constituent parts of that sense of mutual identity: (a) that I recognize the other to be the person he takes himself to be; (b) that he recognizes me to be the person I take myself to be. Within each autonomous sense of identity, there exists the capacity for mutual recognition within a reasonable range of discrepancy and error. And such recognition forms the basis for the experience of ontological security. Ontological insecurity comes about only when there is a lack of such recognition. Laing is emphatic in his conviction that the schizophrenic is a person without hope of mutual recognition. He is a desperate human being. He is *not* loved, neither by mother nor by God. The schizophrenic is one who is "heartbroken" (schiz—broken; phrenos—soul or heart).

The transition from ontological insecurity to ontological security is only possible when love is offered, but without any assurance that the schizophrenic will respond by becoming well. But psychic wholeness is never possible without that self-giving love:

> What is required of us? Understand him? The kernel of the schizo-phrenic's experience of himself must remain incomprehensible to us. As long as we are sane and he is insane, it will remain so. But compre-hension as an effort to reach and grasp him, while remaining within our own world and judging him by our own categories whereby he inevita-bly falls short, is not what the schizophrenic either wants or requires. We have to recognize all the time his distinctiveness and differentness, his separateness and loneliness and despair.[25]

3. THE "TRANSCENDENTAL EXPERIENCE"

Laing agrees with Marcuse that our civilization represses any form of transcendence. The consequence of this repression is that the individ-ual who experiences other dimensions of reality will always be consid-ered mad. And so it has become a fairly standard practice to reject from both a scientific and a clinical perspective any experience which cannot be categorized according to textbook definitions of "normal" human behavior. Laing wants to restore the authentic character of

25. Ibid., p. 38.

"transcendent experience" by demonstrating its validity in the restoration of health to the psychotic. He also wants to demonstrate that such an experience can occur within the psychotic condition. It is ultimately an experience of the divine that Laing is talking about.[26] He has discovered that the psychotic break, which is described in the same terms as the mystical experience, oftentimes evidences a "will towards health." And the result is often a greater understanding of the nature of individual self-consciousness.

When mental illness, insanity, madness, schizophrenia, and psychotic breakdowns are considered as Laing wants to consider them, in existential-social terms, then it becomes easy to recognize the humanity common to both the healthy and the ill personality. For example, human experience may be considered to be "invalidly mad" or "validly mystical." Both forms of behavior, the mad experience and the mystical experience, are considered by society to be deviant forms of behavior. But Laing would insist that both kinds of experience are possible because people experience themselves. That seems to be the criterion which allows for the validity of both the mad and the mystical experience. But Laing does not want to characterize them as examples of socially deviant behavior. Instead he wants to discover the existential meaning of such so-called unusual experiences.

Psychotic experiences are experiences which go beyond the common experiences of man. They are experiences in which the usual "sense" of the world, which is a shared experience, is lost. "Old purposes no longer seem viable," Laing writes; "old meanings are senseless; the distinctions between imagination, dream, external perceptions often seem no longer to apply in the old way. External events may seem magically conjured up. Dreams may seem direct communications from others; imagination may seem to be objective reality."[27] More significant, however, is the fact that the ontological foundations of human existence are shaken. Madness entails a "profound transposition" of the person's relationship to all domains of being. His self-consciousness is a confused experience. Laing speaks about the center of man's experience moving from ego to self. Only the eternal matters now; the temporal sequence of events appears insignificant. This is

26. Laing, *The Politics of Experience,* p. 108.
27. Ibid., p. 109.

then the occasion for that experience which is akin to the mystical experience:

> . . . he often can be to us, through his profound wretchedness and disintegration, the hierophant of the sacred. An exile from the scene of being as we know it, he is an alien, a stranger, signalling to us from the void in which he is foundering, a void which may be peopled by presences that we do not even dream of. . . . But we are distracted from our cozy security by this mad ghost that haunts us with his visions and voices that seem so senseless and of which we feel impelled to rid him, cleanse him, cure him.[28]

What Laing is suggesting is that madness does not have to be only psychic breakdown, it can also be a breakthrough to new vistas of human understanding.

The "transcendental experience," which the psychotic experiences, is also the same kind of experience which helps to explain the origins of the major religions of man. But Laing does not make the mistake of saying that the psychotic experience and the religious experience are one and the same. Most people experience themselves and others in a way which Laing calls egoic. And that means that they experience themselves and the world in a consistent way, identifying themselves and the world over against themselves in a way which is recognizably the same. That experience is corroborated by the experience of others. It is therefore a social experience. And the experience provides man in society with a sense of ontological security. Its validity as experience is self-validating, although its historical and ontological relativity is apparent. That is, we ascribe to a relative historical and social experience an absolute character. But we do so conscious of what we are doing and assured that as we do so, the consequence is the sense of ontological security.

To free oneself from the egoic experience is characteristic of religious and existential philosophies. In Laing's terms, it is "a veil, a film of maya—a dream to Heraclitus, and to Lao-Tzu, the fundamental illusion of all Buddhism, a state of sleep, of death, of socially accepted madness, a womb state to which one has to die, from which one has to be born."[29]

28. Ibid., pp. 109–110.
29. Ibid., p. 113.

The escape from the egoic experience is the focus of Laing's discussion of both madness and mysticism. The person who experiences ego loss, who experiences the move from ontological security to ontological insecurity, often becomes confused and sometimes expresses his confusion in a psychotic way. He may then be adjudged mad, but in reality he may not be ill at all. His entire life may be in the process of changing, of a change which is effecting the reintegration of his whole personality. But, of course, the change may not come about, and he may remain in the confused state.

Laing describes a remarkable incident in the life of a friend, a sculptor, who experienced a profound loss of ego orientation:

> After a period of intense work, and experiencing himself as physically and emotionally exhausted, the voyage began. The sculptor began to see old and familiar things in new and strange ways. "And then I suddenly felt as if time was going back. . . . I looked at the clock and in some way I felt that the clock was reinforcing my own opinion of time going back although I couldn't see the hands moving." He was going back in time. His ego had died and with it the experience of the enhanced significance and relevance of everything.
>
> "I had extraordinary feelings of—living, not only living, but—er—feeling and—er—experiencing everything relating to something. I felt that was—well, something like animal life and so on.
>
> "You know, I was perfectly well aware of myself and aware of the surroundings." The sculptor felt too that he had enhanced power of control over his body and could effect the behavior of others.
>
> "When I went to the hospital, because of this feeling, this intense feeling of being able to—um govern myself, my body and so on. . . ." While in the hospital he even helped with others who were ill.
>
> But what was most characteristic of his experience was that he was on some kind of enormous journey "a fantastic journey, and it seemed that I had got an understanding of things which I'd been trying to understand for a long time, problems of good and evil and so on, and that I had solved it in as much that I had come to the conclusion, with all the feelings that I had at the time, that I was more—more than I had always imagined myself."[30]

30. Ibid., Chapter 7.

He had feelings of God, or gods, "of beings which are far above us, capable of dealing with the situation that I was incapable of dealing with, that were in charge and were running things." The gods were related to an ordering of the universe or were related to stages in an evolutionary development of man.

But then he decided to come back. He opened himself to the possibilities of a new understanding of his life. He was in a padded cell at the time: "So they left the door open, and I remember going through that night struggling with—with something that wanted to —some sort of—curiosity or willingness to open myself to—experiencing—this, and the panic and the insufficiency of spirit that would enable me to experience it." In a way, he recapitulated what Kierkegaard called "choosing oneself in despair." He then realized that the experience was over, the drama came to an end! And the sculptor acknowledged that he was "capable of running things now." In reflecting about his experience later with Laing, he recognized the importance of other people, that there "should be other people who sort of look after you," and that "the thing that gave me comfort sometimes was the fact that other people were taking it" (in reference to a frightening experience at sea when he was a young man). He came out of the hospital after ten days, the journey ended, and realized that his world was much more real than it had ever been before. "I could see the bad things and the good things and all that. I was much more aware."

Laing is convinced that such a voyage is not what man needs to be cured of but is itself a natural way of dealing with the state of human alienation which society labels normal. It is the process by which the self heals the self.

It is this "other world," the world beyond the normal world, which Laing sees as a real world, a world whose reality is different from the psychologically normal world of dreams, neuroses, and perception. This is the world in which the ego is broken up or is destroyed by the one-dimensional alien world in which man lives. It might be through the voyage into this world that a reintegration of personality occurs.

But the odds are great against such a voyage ever taking place. Sanity is defined by our society as man's capacity to adapt to an "external world of human collectivities." The inner world, the world of direct personal awareness, is by definition suspect. The inner world is "our way of seeing the external world and all those realities that have no 'external,' 'objective' presence—imagination, dreams, fantasies, trances, the realities of contemplative and meditative states, realities that modern man for the most part has not the slightest direct awareness of."[31] Laing wants to reintroduce the biblical motif of the direct experience of God, or to put it in the author's own terms, of the immediate illumination of the source of all reality and all meaning: "There is everything to suggest that man experienced God. Faith was never a matter of believing he existed, but of trusting in the Presence that was experienced and known to exist as a self-validating datum."[32]

For Laing, to experience God and to be truly sane are one and the same experience. True sanity means the dissolution of the false ego ("that false self competently adjusted to our alienated social reality") and the emergence of a new functioning ego ("the ego now being the servant of the divine and not its betrayer").

B. ANALYSIS AND CRITIQUE

It is obvious that Laing is expressing a conception of transcendence or several conceptions of transcendence that are similar to what Jews and Christians understand by transcendence. For Laing, transcendence is a functional concept, related to man's relationship to his world and to his fellow men. As such, Laing's understanding of transcendence places man in the context of personal human relationships. These relationships become determinative for who man is, for his consciousness of himself, and more crucially, for the condition of his mental health. Furthermore, Laing rejects the tired distinction between the inner and outer man and allows man to experience "profounder" dimensions of his selfhood in fantasies and mystical experiences.

Laing has described in convincing ways the nature of man's alienation from himself and from his neighbor. And it is this alienated state

31. Ibid., p. 115.
32. Ibid., p. 118.

with which man must come to terms. The alienation is of an ontological character; that is, it affects man's ability to develop his true humanity. Ontological insecurity characterizes man in the modern world. Those persons who cannot find "creative" ways of dealing with ontological insecurity become schizophrenic, which for Laing becomes an authentic way to deal with the absurdities of modern life. Man's capacity for transcendence, Laing maintains, allows him to enter into a loving and giving relationship with another human being:

> We are both acted upon, changed for good or ill by other men; and we are agents who act upon others to affect them in different ways. Each of us is the other to the other.[33]

The relationship to the other, that relationship which creates being from nonbeing, that relationship that expresses the divine activity of *creatio ex nihilo,* is what Laing calls the transcendent character of the self. It is an act of what Jews and Christians call "agapeic love," the giving of oneself to another in a relationship which creates a being where before there was no being. But persons are also capable of what Laing has called "transpersonal invalidation," which is the denial of another's humanity by the manipulation of that relationship.

Transcendence is, therefore, for Laing a personalistic category which allows a miracle to occur, the creation of another self. In the creation of another self, the person's own selfhood is affirmed. Laing is not too far removed from Luther's characterization of the redeemed man, whose heart is no longer turned in upon itself but is directed outward to the neighbor. One's ego has been affirmed by God. And because one has experienced the deliverance from bondage to the self, one is then free to devote one's time and energy in the service of others. Laing is here expressing profoundly what the Christian affirms about man in relation to the neighbor.

1. LAING'S CONCEPT OF "ONTOLOGICAL SECURITY"

Laing's conception of ontological security introduces a number of theological and psychoanalytic problems. Ontological security provides man with an orientation in time and space. As a result, the

33. Ibid., pp. 25–26.

ordinary circumstances of everyday life do not constitute a deadly threat to his existence. And Laing wants to designate infancy as the period when ontological security is usually introduced. The baby's point of view is one in which he feels alive and real and has a sense of being an entity in time and space. For Laing, ontological security, therefore, has a biological and physical genesis.

But ontological security and insecurity ought to have more than a biological root. To be oriented in time and space ought to have a theological root; that is, there ought to be an ideological and spiritual complement to the biological genesis of security. Ontological security is not the result of the transposition of the person's physical environment, as Laing knows, nor is it in every case the consequence of the sophisticated therapeutic session. Ontological security comes about when a person *feels* secure, when he experiences another who has given himself in love to him. But then he is really secure, his physical environment has dramatically changed, his mental health has been restored. A miracle has occurred. And it has occurred because he has "blown his mind"; he has entered into a world in which miracles are possible, in which the empirical is no longer counted as absolute, and in which other worlds open up to him. But to allow oneself to be transported into another world suggests the "eyes of faith," to see that it is possible, to engage oneself in the "voyage of discovery," to allow oneself to discover dimensions of reality which transcend in time and space the mundane material world.

The Christian notion of mental health is even more radical than Laing has recognized. The Christian affirms that man has been given mental wholeness as a consequence of the Incarnation, that is, that he is really physiologically as well as psychologically secure. But his security is not dependent upon some clever manipulation of his environment or his psyche. Man is secure because God in Christ has secured the self, and he has done so at great expense to himself. Man's security is dependent neither upon vague notions of spiritual harmony nor upon concepts of phantasmagoric oneness. He is secure because of the historical humanity of Jesus Christ, who has come to be with man and to save him from selfishness and self-indulgence. Man's selfhood is secure, not because he struggles to make it so and sometimes is capable of achieving selfhood. His selfhood is secure because it has been assured in the gift of God's love in the Incarnation.

2. LAING'S IMPLICIT MYSTICISM

There are several ways to "blow one's mind." Laing suggests a number of meanings to the expression: the self's "voyage of discovery," or the self which redirects itself in time and space, thereby achieving ontological security. Another meaning is found in the mystic's experience of the realm of oneness beyond or outside the normal external, empirical world. Laing wants to lead his patients to that state where there can be gotten "illumination from the inner." Modern alienated man is in a state of darkness, which Laing defines as "a state of sin," or alienation or estrangement from the "inner light." He makes a telling point when he describes man's experience of God as a self-validating datum. In the past, man did not need to be convinced that God existed. He believed because he experienced God and "trusted in the Presence that was experienced." Laing is on safe theological grounds when he argues in this way. The conceptual knowledge of God is far removed from the experience of the living presence of God. And Laing recommends to his neighbor faith in the living presence of God.

Jews and Christians ought to be encouraged by Laing's call for a renewal of a vital and experiential faith in the living presence of God. But Jews and Christians ought to recognize too the limitations of the mystical kind of religious experience that Laing proposes. Laing sets in opposition to one another the conceptual character of contemporary religiosity and the experiential character of classical Christian mysticism. He calls for man to rediscover ecstacy, to experience the spirit, to allow for the dissolution of the normal ego, to permit the emergence of the "inner" archetypal mediators of divine power, and to experience the eventual reestablishment of a new kind of ego functioning.[34] My argument is not with the intention of Laing to evoke ego health by means of what he calls "the transcendental experience" but with his attempt to align the transcendental experience solely to the mystical experience. A number of problems are evident. First, in the Western mystical tradition it is highly unlikely that the mystical experience can be subjected to clinical controls. The mystic's experi-

34. Ibid., pp. 118–119.

ence is spontaneous and uncontrolled, often occurring when there is least reason to anticipate it: its genesis belongs to the prerogative of God and not to the spiritual manipulation of man. Second, the mystical experience can only be related tangentially to mental health; that is to say, there is no guarantee that there will be a new ego orientation as a consequence of the mystic's experience. In fact, if the new ego orientation is directed solely to God, it may be difficult to get the mystic to communicate directly with his neighbors. Moreover, it may be impossible for him ever to speak about the experience of illumination or oneness or unity or whatever. His experience may ultimately not have anything to do with human relationships and may be always a private and nondescriptive experience. Laing, of course, recognizes this fact. What I am concerned about is the development of any kind of criteria which would tie the mystical experience irrevocably to mental health. The experience of the mystic is of an intangible and ineffable reality. The expression of that experience cannot by its own nature be translated into categories of another experience or into those which would be intelligible to the psychoanalytic practitioner. But Laing is aware too of this limitation:

> The "ego" is the instrument for living in *this* world. If the "ego" is broken up, or destroyed (by the insurmountable contradictions of certain life situations, by toxins, chemical changes, etc.) then the person may be exposed to other worlds, "real" in different ways from the more familiar territory of dreams, imagination, perception or phantasy.[35]

How to speak about the reality of the world becomes a problem for anyone seriously concerned with evaluating the experiences of life in a meaningful way. To allow the experiences to speak for themselves might be the most adequate means by which to deal with the experiences. But then one cannot pretend that one has found a method for evaluating the experiences or developed categories that allow for a universe of discourse so that the experiences might be shared and communicated.

35. Ibid., pp. 114–115.

3. THE PANTHEISTIC CHARACTER OF LAING'S CONCEPT OF TRANSCENDENCE

The inherent pantheism in Laing's "transcendental experience" invites some confusion. If God is the reality behind the "inner world," then psychological anarchy breaks loose. And that is so because one has given the character of absoluteness to the inner experience; one has equated it with God. It is therefore self-authenticating and self-validating. Laing develops a hierarchy between the outer and inner worlds. The outer is the world of the material, of the imprisonment of the senses; it is illusory; it is the outer world which embraces the alienation of so much of contemporary life. The inner world, on the other hand, is the world of ecstacy, of freedom, of authentic human experiences; it is the world which participates in the life of God. But to develop such a hierarchy presents a totalitarianism of another sort: if the spiritual world is the only true world and if God is on the side of that world, then the clever manipulation of human emotions becomes possible, and moreover, it becomes the grandest achievement of man, the introduction of authentic life where there is only alienation. By so doing, Laing allows for the crudest kind of exploitation of the human psyche and the cheapest sort of sensitivity manipulation as well as the random introduction of new spiritual saviors, the army of maharishis who flood the alienated suburban communities, and the development of new and forceful and highly financed sectarian developments. And he has allowed this to happen in the face of the task he has established for himself, the liberation of man from the falsity and manipulation and shoddiness of man's phony world.

God cannot be characterized in pantheistic terms if mental health is the objective of the transrational mystical experience. God must continue to function in a historic, concrete, and personalistic way. God acts historically to save all intellectual and psychotherapeutic systems from intellectual and spiritual exploitation; concretely, in order to establish a standard by which to evaluate the most current so-called manifestation of the divine presence; personalistically, to permit a relationship between persons who are in the process of coming into being. But God also functions in a delimiting way in order to relegate all manipulation of the psyche to the realm of manipulation and clearly not to the activity of God.

It is instructive to read of Herbert Marcuse's rejection of Norman O. Brown's mysticism in *Love's Body*. Brown envisioned an absolute, or a totality, a cosmic whole that swallowed up all parts and divisions, all tensions, and all needs. Marcuse responded to Brown in a manner which denied all pantheisms: "For such a totality does not exist in any sense or nonsense, and should not even be the vision of the free imagination because it is the negation of all freedom, and of all happiness (at least human happiness)." Marcuse's criticism of pantheism is based upon a political criterion: "You know," Marcuse writes, "that the political fight is the fight for the whole; not the mystical whole, but the very unmystical, antagonistic whole of our life and that of our children—the only life that is."[36] There can be no new life, no new experience of human life, until the deception and exploitation of society is ultimately broken. Only when there is a political revolution can there develop a new self-consciousness. What Brown has done is to mystify the establishment, that is, to give to it and to the means by which to deal with it a mystical character. But what happens actually is that the establishment swallows up the mystic. He counts for nothing. He no longer has the capacity to recognize his exploitation.

And I am certain that Laing's mystic would not recognize the nature of that form of psyche-exploitation either. Anything goes—as long as the psyche is mystified. The same environmental conditions that created, or at least abetted, the development of the estranged ego go on. And happily so, because the self is in union with God. There is peace and joy and happiness. But such an experience can be as much of a sham as the emotions which Laing violently lashed out against in his description of the alienated society. "Flights of mystical insight" are legitimate means of dealing with a disturbed soul and a perverse society *only* when the returned individual can now deal concretely and positively with his psyche and with his society.

36. Herbert Marcuse, *Negations: Essays in Critical Theory* (Boston: Beacon Press, 1968), pp. 241 and 243.

4

TRANSCENDENCE
AS *FUTURE*
—ERNST BLOCH

A. EXPOSITION

Ernst Bloch (along with George Lukács) belongs to a group of Marxist thinkers known as the "philosophical left opposition." His particular effort has been to restore the humanistic and eschatological character of Marx in the face of its practical and theoretical collapse in the hands of the Second International. Bloch is an avowed atheist, yet in a peculiar way he is a profoundly religious thinker. He is a loner, someone who defies categorization. His intellectual itinerary has taken him through the period of late Imperial Germany, World War I, the crashed hopes of revolution in the postwar years, the rise and fall of Weimar, Stalinism, an emigration to the United States (to Philadelphia), then to East Germany, and finally to Tübingen in West Germany. Bloch is characterized by one of his sympathetic interpreters in the following way:

> Specifically, Bloch is a product and producer of the wave of religious socialism, anarcho-communitarian mysticism, anti-capitalist culture-criticism, and Expressionist art that erupted from within a sector of the Central European intelligentsia—first, prior to World War I, in anticipation of a coming apocalypse and redemption; then, in the 1917 years, as the wildly vibrant expression of real revolutionary upheavals and hopes. Bloch is unique among those who were part of the eruption not simply by virtue of the fact that he has survived, but because he has sustained and preserved that messianic, eschatological, utopian move-

ment as the foundation of his thought—insisting now, as then, on its roots in humanity's telos.[1]

Bloch is a Marxist revolutionary in the same sense that Erich Fromm is a Marxist revolutionary. They look at the younger Marx of the 1844 *Philosophical and Political Manuscripts* as the protagonist of the total liberation of the human spirit from the domination of economic pressures. Marx is the architect of man's introduction into a world in which he is "at home" with himself, with his neighbor, and with a "resurrected nature." Bloch complements Marx's profound humanism with an emphasis upon the eschatological and utopian elements of the Marxist system.

Bloch's work, especially in *Das Prinzip Hoffnung (I–III),* is an attempt to decipher the nature of the human consciousness, that consciousness which in much of the Marxist literature is tied so intimately to the processes of economic development. Bloch has discerned and described the human "essence" which lies behind the economic forms of the bourgeois capitalistic societies. But for Bloch that human consciousness includes the religious consciousness, which he rejects in all of its institutional and ecclesiastical forms. However, the religious consciousness in its *sui generis* form he can accept.

Bloch accepts Marx's statement that "religious suffering is the expression of real suffering and at the same time the protest against real suffering. Religion is the sigh of the oppressed creature, the heart of a heartless world, as it is the spirit of spiritless conditions."[2] Bloch contends that religion is a fundamental part of the human essence and is not, as with Marx, expressive of man's alienation from his true humanity. The religious consciousness expresses a dimension of man's humanity which cannot be described solely in economic and political categories.[3] Real social revolution cannot come, Bloch argues, without an acknowledgment of the "spiritual interiority" of revolution itself. Revolution cannot mean the realignment of social and eco-

1. Paul Breines, "Bloch Magic," *Continuum* 7, no. 4 (Winter 1970):620.
2. Karl Marx, "Toward the Critique of Hegel's Philosophy of Law: Introduction," *Writings of the Young Marx on Philosophy and Society,* trans. and ed. L. D. Easton and K. H. Guddat (New York: Doubleday-Anchor Books, 1967), p. 250.
3. Both Harvey Cox in his Foreword to the English translation of *Man on His Own,* trans. E. B. Ashton (New York: Herder and Herder, 1970) and Jürgen Moltmann in his Introduction to the same volume acknowledge Bloch's influence on the development of their own theological position.

nomic forces; they are nothing but the system of forms of the "reified objectivity of this real life." Bloch writes:

> . . . history is a polyrhythmic creation in which not only the social self-discovery of the still hidden social man, but also the artistic, religious, metaphysical self-discovery of the secret, transcendental man is a consciousness of being, a *new* depth-relation of being.[4]

Bloch's concept of transcendence is tied up with his analysis of the religious man. The oft-quoted phrase from Bloch, "*S* is not yet *P*," offers a clue to his conception of transcendence. No subject already has its adequate predicate. A new logic is necessary to deal with the fact that change is the only permanent thing with which we can deal. Reality is not yet actuality; the world as it is is not yet the *regnum humanum.*[5] Religion is for Bloch the awesome abyss between what is and what is to come. Religion describes the hopes and longings that man has for a future which has not yet come into being. Religious man is the man who hopes, the man who can peer into the future with confidence not because of a certainty of what will occur but because of what there is yet to be accomplished. And it is man who, in the process, grows increasingly aware of himself and of what he can become. Transcendence is that experience of that which is not yet fully come into being.

Bloch could never be thought of as a churchman. That is certainly true. But it is also true that Bloch has had a profound impact upon contemporary developments in Christian theological thought and ecclesiastical reformulation. The church makes its peace with the past or adjusts its expectations to the principle of expediency. But the truly religious man rejects the self-satisfied institutions and projects himself with hope toward the unrealized future. And so man envisages the transcendent (the ideal) in the midst of the actual (the real).

1. BLOCH'S UNORTHODOX MARXISM

Bloch must be considered a Marxist deviationist because his thinking does not conform to the standards dictated by Soviet dialectical

---

4. Ernst Bloch, "Aktualität und Utopie. Zu Lukács' Geschichte und Klassenbewusstsein," in Paul Breines' "Bloch Magic," p. 623.

5. Cf. the review of *Man on His Own* by David Gross in *Continuum* 7, no. 4 (Winter 1970).

materialism. He rejects the narrowly conceived economism of the orthodox Marxist. He refuses to write in the deadly "philosophese" of his confreres, and his style is filled with imaginative metaphors and provocative symbols. He has put speculation and poetry back into Marxist ideology. But his own version of Marxism is characterized by a utopianism which he insists is found in the young Marx.

Bloch refers to Marxism as "near to being a Critique of Pure Reason for which no Critique of Practical Reason has yet been written."[6] This appears to be a key passage in the whole Blochian corpus. Bloch conceives of his own philosophical task as that of contributing to the development of a "Marxist Critique of Practical Reason." To this end, he emphasizes the teleological and eschatological character of dialectical materialism: "Throughout all the movements and goals of world transformation," Bloch writes, "there has been a desire to make room for life, for the attainment of a divine essence, for men to integrate themselves at last, in a millenium, with human kindness, freedom, and the light of the *telos*. "[7] Bloch rejects the narrow Marxist concentration on economics as "the system of the forms of objectivity of real life." Marxism has an inherent *telos* which too many of Marx's followers have forgotten or rejected in favor of the economic interpretation of real life. It is Bloch's task to introduce that notion again. As he does so, he introduces religious categories of a Jewish and Christian sort which complement his basic Marxist position. It is for this reason that he has attracted widespread interest among the theologians of the Christian tradition and that he has alienated himself from the more normative and orthodox Marxist interpreters. David Gross in a review of *Man on His Own* summarizes Bloch's thought as an amalgam of "the concrete utopianism of the early Marx, mixed in with a dash of Joachim di Fiore and Saint John of the Apocalypse."[8]

Bloch reveals his Marxist orientation and his revisionistic position

6. Ernst Bloch, *Man on His Own* (New York: Herder and Herder, 1970) p. 39.
7. Ibid.
8. David Gross, review of *Man on His Own*, p. 627. (Bloch's own study of the left-wing Protestant reformer Thomas Münzer (1921) reveals what Bloch himself regards as "revolutionary romanticism." *Das Prinzip Hoffnung*, Vols. I-III (1954 – 1959), reflects the more mature Bloch.

in a crucial chapter entitled "Karl Marx, Death and the Apocalypse" in the volume *Man on His Own*. The state, Bloch argues, exists to provide economic efficiencies. If it cannot perform this function, it becomes obsolete. In the modern state there is no real concern for individuals. Private property is the culprit. Legal protection is a fiction. Law becomes the instrument of the ruling classes. The economic order can be regulated by means of legal formalisms. Both the lawyer and the judge lack any concern to get at the truth. Even when the state gets involved in the investigation and prosecution of crime it is a sham operation and functions to protect the interests of the ruling classes. If there were no property, then there would be no need for this kind of arbitrary functioning of the law in society.

The coercively structured state becomes in time the war-state. It inevitably must ally itself with those interests which believe themselves challenged by other societies and other ideologies. The state, Bloch argues, has "unveiled itself as a heathenish, satanic, coercive being, in itself, its power unchecked, its rewriting of the historical past justifying any kind of barbaric behavior."[9]

The state may continue to function for a time in a Bolshevist form, but it must ultimately "wither away," which for Bloch means "its transformation into an international regulator of production and consumption, an immense apparatus set up to control inessentials and no longer containing, or capable of attracting, anything of import."[10] Under socialism, the state is an administrative agency which supports different nations and cultures. Its only reason for being is "the clarifying frictionless operation of its regulative method in the midst of illogical life."[11]

2. THE CRITICISM OF THE STATE

a. THE ALLIANCE OF THE PROLETARIAT AND THE PHILOSOPHER.
The agent of revolution is the oppressed wage slave, who looks at revolution as a means of economic elevation. The motive for the

9. Bloch, *Man on His Own*, p. 33.
10. Ibid.
11. Ibid.

revolution is the proletariat's private interest. His ambition to live a better life is the motivating force behind the revolutionary goal of the dissolution of the capitalistic society. To this proletarian class belongs "the heritage of all freedom; the beginning of world history (after pre-history); the first genuine, total revolution; the end of all class struggles; and deliverance from the materialism of class interests as such."[12] The revolution Bloch envisions necessitates an alliance between the poor (those individuals who have nothing to look forward to) and the philosopher (who may be the ideological architect of the future). "Philosophy," Bloch writes, "is no longer philosophy unless it is dialectical and materialistic. . . . But also, dialectical materialism cannot be such unless it is philosophical, i.e., it must proceed toward broad and open horizons."[13] The "broad and open horizons" include, according to Bloch, the realization of philosophy by the abrogation of the proletariat. But the proletariat cannot abrogate itself without the realization of philosophy. Philosophy adds an ideology to the self-interested ambitions of the proletariat class ("egotism" in Marxist terminology). That ideology is characterized ultimately by the moral purity of communism. But Bloch feels certain that this alliance between the poor proletariat and the philosopher is an illustration of Marx's uncritical Hegelianism. There is historically an invariable contradiction between the interests of the individual and the concept of the good. Bloch knows this, as do Christian realists. But it seems as if Marx was oblivious to this fact. To conceive of an alliance between the self-interested wage-slave, whose historical ambition is to effect a revolution so that his earthly status in life will be changed, and the philosopher, who conceives of the ideological establishment of the common good, and not to see that there might be a variance between the two is to accept the Hegelian dialectic uncritically. Marx outdoes Hegel in his naive acceptance of the historicizing of the self-interested proletariat in the communist society. So Bloch argues. Bloch insists that the problem of the "subjective" will of the proletariat and the "objective" ideal of the philosopher and the relationship between the

12. Ibid., p. 34.
13. Ernst Bloch, *Subjekt-Objekt: Erklänterung zu Hegel* (Frankfurt am Main: Suhrkamp, 1962), p. 519. Quoted in Paul Piccone, "Bloch's Marxism," *Continuum* 7, no. 4 (Winter 1970): 630.

two must be thought out metaphysically. Marx failed to do this. Bloch
wants to attempt an alliance:

> History is a hard and a mixed voyage; there is only a chance that
> long-continued *activity* will turn into time, into its own *objectivity*—
> that it will change and transform time into a point of least resistance,
> or indeed into an allied private dynamics of objectivity.[14]

b. CRITICISM OF MARXISM.   Marx conceived of the evils within
capitalism as derivative of its economic base. As he did so, he separated the economic from the psychological. It is not man's consciousness that determined his existence, but it is the other way around: it
is his economic existence that determined his consciousness. Bloch
believes that this fundamental Marxist idea, the basis for Marx's
scientific socialism, is ultimately barren and fundamentally wrong:

> Man does not live by bread alone. Outward things, no matter how
> extensive their importance and our need to attend to them, are merely
> suggestive, not creative. People, not things and not the mighty course
> of events outside ourselves (which Marx falsely places above us), write
> history. His determinism applies to the economic future, to the neces-
> sary economic-institutional change; but the new man, the leap, the
> power of love and light, and morality itself, are not yet accorded the
> requisite independence in the definitive social order.[15]

Bloch wants to make room for the soul and religious faith within the
Marxist dialectic. To do so he must restore the utopian dimension
within Marx's ideology. Bloch believes that a utopian perspective
would give a moral and cultural dimension to the new socialist society: "It [socialism] must result in an equally 'correct' *a priori* way
of thinking and of culture that cannot be defined simply as 'free
thinking,' as the banal atheism whose ideals socialists have taken over
from bourgeois philistines."[16] Bloch opposes the Marxist atheistic
position which offers nothing more than a pleasure-filled heaven on
earth and the ideals filled with heart, conscience, mind, and spirit, the
communion of all living, the brotherhood of man—all realizable on

14. Bloch, *Man on His Own,* pp. 35–38.
15. Ibid., p. 37.
16. Ibid.

this earth. This is Bloch's historical ambition: to make room for life, to attain the divine essence, to integrate man into a millenium with human kindness, freedom, and the light of the *telos*.[17] And basic to Bloch's position is an anthropology which describes man as a being who is not yet what he might become. Man is therefore the "one who hopes." His essential nature is that of creative expectation of that which has not yet come into being. The content of the "not yet" is that future which allows man to be free.

c. THE ESCHATOLOGICAL CHARACTER OF MARXISM.   Bloch uses the language of religion, especially the eschatological language of Judaism and Christianity, to describe the political character of Marxism. He sees Marxism as an essential part of the eschatological development of the great religious traditions of the West. But he wants finally to rescue religion from the idolatry of its institutional practitioners. "Marxism becomes the theory and religion becomes its practice"; together they form two independent but complementary parts of the total humanizing process which only together can become historically realizable:

> Thus the distant totality of Utopia presents the picture of a building without a single economically profitable part: with everyone producing what he can; everyone consuming what he needs; everyone, according to the degree of his contribution, of his moral and intellectual ministry, openly taking, and taken on, mankind's way home through the dark of the world.[18]

Bloch wants to effect a unity of the Marxist socialist economic ideal with the historical realization of the society of the new church ("an a priori socialist-oriented Church facing new contents of revelation"). Such a combination can effect a new social economy organized along communist lines, a classless and nonviolent society. Bloch compares such a society with the kingdom of brotherly love. In this regard he quotes from the Zohar:

> Consequently there are two degrees of action, the works and the orders of prayer; the works serve the outward perfection of the worlds, but the

17. Ibid., p. 39.
18. Ibid., p. 40.

prayers serve to make one world contained in the other and to lift them upward.[19]

3. JUDAISM AND CHRISTIANITY AS THE *PRACTICE* OF MARXISM

The conception of the new life (the formulation of the *incipit vita nova*) as a historical event came into the world through the Bible. That is Bloch's claim: ". . . as if before Jesus there has been nothing in any way really new, but only longing for, and suggestions and expectations of, this one new thing."[20] Bloch is speaking about the biblical concept of the miraculous actions of God within history to effect the new in the midst of the old, to bring about the renewal of creation so that "not one stone would be left upon another." He is conscious of the decidedly historical character of the events of the Creation and the Incarnation and conceives of them as essential events in the deliverance of man from bondage.

But there is a difference between the Jewish-Christian and the Egyptian and Babylonian formulations of messianism. The Egyptians and the Babylonians looked forward to the miraculous ruler who would come at the end of time. And the Persian Zoroastrian conceived of salvation in terms of the return of Zoroaster. The Romans too, especially at the time of Caesar Augustus, looked to the end of history and the advent of salvation as events related to one another. But Judaism and Christianity affirmed that "the setting of the *content of life itself* [was to be found] in the ultimate life begun [the essential *vita* of the *incipit vita ultima*]."[21] Jews and Christians were waiting for the new life that would mean an end to bondage on this earth. This new life would be a breakthrough; a totally new kind of life would be brought into being. But that new life was established as a classless society. And it was this society which was such an integral part of the utopian dreams of Judaism and early Christianity. "Behold, I make all things new" continues to be the clarion call of the utopian visions

19. Ibid., p. 72.
20. Ibid., p. 76; cf. also pp. 118 ff. and Bloch's discussion of "Christian Social Utopias."
21. Ibid., p. 78.

of both Judaism and Christianity. Bloch appears almost in the role of the Christian apologist when he writes of the unique new society which Christ would bring into being:

> The initiator of the ultimate age . . . was a son of man who had nowhere to lay his head, and whose message the ruling class answered with the cross. Not Caesar but his opposite established the new kingdom: and not as an empire but as a mystical democracy. Only as such has the "Behold, I make all things new" of the book of Revelation continued to operate in all heretics who revolt against "Babylon the Great." The full scope and resonance of that voice rings out from Patmos and down the ages, long, long undimmed: even in the tribune Cola di Rienzo in the non-aristocratic stirrings of the classical Renaissance; but even more in Joachim di Fiore and his prophecies, and in Thomas Münzer —who took them quite seriously as prophecies of the Commune into which Christ would be resolved.[22]

Bloch views the messianic promise of the new age, fulfilled in the person of Jesus of Nazareth, as containing the authentic ingredients of the Communist revolution: the emergence of a classless society and the creation of the commune of the liberated, which is the cataclysmic destruction of all tyrannical powers, and the new creation of the truly human being. Nonbiblical views of the end of history, which Bloch calls, "patrician eschatologies," cannot adequately describe the transition from the old eon to the new as the cessation of bondage. "This was the sole watchword of messianism throughout the centuries that followed: liberation from the burden of oppression and the stench of decay; a breakthrough into fresh air and open spaces; the promotion of a humane future together with a humanism of nature that makes this messianism the *a priori* of every actually revolutionary rebirth or new birth, including the Renaissance itself."[23]

Bloch makes the same point in his discussion of the "Biblical Resurrection and Apocalypse." Immortality in the Old Testament originated with Daniel (about 160 B.C.). Belief in immortality was related to the notion of the justice of God on this earth. Life after death was to make up for the judgment which was missing on earth. In Bloch's

22. Ibid., p. 79.
23. Ibid., p. 80.

view, Daniel 12:2, "And many of them that sleep in the dust of the earth shall awake, some to everlasting life, and some to shame and everlasting contempt," is the background of Jesus' teaching about the Resurrection and Judgment (Matt. 11:24; Luke 10:12) and seemed to be part of Christian teaching from the beginning of the Church (Heb. 6:1 ff.). Jesus is designated as the "bread of life"; his victory was assured as he himself was the resurrection and the life. He was the bearer of the second or heavenly life over against the death of hell. Deliverance from death was the message he brought and by his own death and resurrection he assured life for all of his followers. In this context, Bloch quotes John 6:54, "Whoso eateth my flesh, and drinketh my blood, hath eternal life; and I will raise him up at the last day"; and also John 11:25, "I am the resurrection, and the life; he that believeth in me, though he were dead, yet shall he live."[24]

The identification of the believer with Christ in his death was raised to an archetypal character in the subsequent history of the Church. The doubts about divine justice were related to the concept of retribution on the last day. Christ, who was crucified, is the Christ who will also judge (cf. Rev. 19:11ff.). The Church, of course, used the event of the apocalypse as an instrument to intimidate believers and non-believers alike. However, the archetypal character of Christ's triumph over death persisted. The dead would come back to life at the time of the great roll call.

These were notions that fanned the fires of revolution for the burdened and oppressed throughout all of Christian history. Nothing would remain unavenged! So was the faith of the Christian who conceived of the end of history as the vindication of God's justice. The martyrs and the slaves will return as the victors and the avengers. The kingdom which is to come is for the living. Because Christ was raised from the dead, therefore all shall live. The apocalypse of Saint John is unequivocal in its reference to the organic and materialistic character of that new life (Rev. 22:1 ff.). Light is equal to life; the pure castle of light is paradise. And Christ's ascension was the triumphant introduction of all men to a residency in that realm of life.

24. Bloch also refers to the Christocentric character of the restoration of life, John 6:49,51; II Timothy 1:19; John 5:26.

But it is Bloch's conviction throughout his exegesis of the Old and New Testaments that the teaching about resurrection and the kingdom introduced a utopian ideal into the consciousness of Western man, an ideal of the transformed life *within* history. He locates the advent of that life at the end of history, at the time when the kingdom will be established, when the utopian ideal shall be historicized. But it is always a historical realization that he is pointing to. The perversity of the Church made heaven an impossible ideal beyond history, but the persistence of the notion of the new life shattered the intellectual and institutional bonds that Christianity attempted to put about it. "Behold I make all things new," refers (for Bloch) to the practical realization of the dreams of a people imprisoned by the barbarity of past oppressions. The apocalypse reveals nothing but organic things: "And he showed me a pure river of water of life, clear as crystal, proceeding out of the throne of God and of the Lamb. In the midst of the street of it, and on either side of the river, was there the tree of life, which bore twelve manners of fruit, and yielded her fruit every month." (Rev. 22:1 ff)

Bloch's basic understanding of the biblical idea of community is that of a utopian kingdom, in which an enslaved people are released from bondage. But it is a historical kingdom, which is realized in time, even though it is in projected time, as a future event. In this connection, Bloch asks us to consider the life of Moses. He is called by Yahweh to lead an enslaved people away from Egypt and into the promised land. Moses killed an Egyptian and therefore had to leave the country. The first act of the founder of the Jewish community precipitated his departure from the country. For Bloch, that fact is decisive. The world was turned upside down; the normally anticipated human relationships were radically altered. Moses' God became the God of a liberated people. The Exodus was therefore an exodus from bondage to liberation. Bloch indicates, too, that the liberated community was a primitive, communistic type of society, in which there was no private property. Private property becomes possible only in the land of Canaan. It was there where nomadic communal life came to an end. In its place came the wonders and agonies of the agrarian and city-dwelling stages of economic and social development. Crafts and trades emerged, but also slavery and class distinctions, and prosperity and poverty. The prophets appeared in the midst of all of this, denouncing the exploitation and injustices of the ruling classes. And they developed plans for a social utopia, modeled on the earlier nomadic communistic societies. Bloch argues in traditional Marxist fashion:

> Apostacy (from Yahweh) meant turning from a sort of pre-capitalistic Yahweh to Baal, and also to that master's Yahweh who had conquered Baal at the price of turning himself into a God of luxury.[25]

Yahweh is against capitalism and the class distinctions and the conspicuous consumption it promotes. But he is *for* the primitive bedouin type of community, in which there are no private property and no distinctions in class. The prophet, therefore, as Yahweh's representative, must call an apostate people back to the justice that prevailed in the primitive community (cf.Amos 5:21,24 and Isa. 5:7 ff., Isa. 13:11 ff., and Isa. 42:22). The prophet calls upon Yahweh to punish the evil accumulators of capital. Yahweh promises that he will bring about the time of universal happiness and wealth, which Bloch conceives of as "socialist wealth":

> He, every one that thirsteth, come ye to the waters, and he that hath no money; come ye, buy and eat; yea, come, buy wine and milk without money and without price.   (Isa. 55:1)

The socialistic society will also be pacifistic, on an international scale. Bloch refers to both Micah and Isaiah on this point:

> And he shall judge among many people, and rebuke strong nations afar off; and they shall beat their swords into plowshares, and their spears into pruninghooks; nation shall not lift up sword against nation, neither shall they learn war anymore. But they shall sit every man under his vine and under his fig tree; and none shall make them afraid.   (Mic. 4:2–4; Isa. 2:3 ff.)

This is the original model of the pacifistic international which forms the basis for all subsequent Christian utopias.

The New Testament then begins with a distinctive messianic note. The promised land appeared less than it was supposed to be. Class

25. Bloch, *Man on His Own*, p. 119.

distinctions still remained. Roman society, with its rampant disregard for the sufferings of the lower classes, prospered. The prophets could now be called "agitators." The God of the prophets became an ancient tribal deity, no longer related to modern society. John the Baptist and Jesus preached to the lowest classes of people and promised them an end to their miseries (Matt. 3:10). Jesus' message is not for the ruling classes, nor was it an otherworldly message. Bloch refers to Matthew who announces the messiah-king who will terminate all forms of suffering upon earth (Matt. 11:25–30). Indeed, Bloch argues accurately that the terms "this world" and the "other world" were never meant to be geographical designations dividing this world from the next, but rather, they referred to the present eon and the future eon, a succession in time on the same stage, on this earth.[26] The "other world" was the utopian earth with a utopian heaven above:

> For, behold, I create new heavens and a new earth; and the former shall not be remembered, nor come into mind. (Isa. 65:17)

Bloch comments: "The goal was not a beyond after death, where the angels sing; it was the terrestrial as well as supraterrestrial kingdom of love, with its first enclave already constituted by the original community. Not until after the catastrophe of the cross was the kingdom of the other world interpreted as lying in the beyond."[27]

Jesus' crucifixion could only be interpreted as a catastrophe. Jesus' outcry on the cross would appear to substantiate Bloch's estimation. The early acceptance of the religion of Jesus by the ruling Roman classes was prompted by the desire of the Neros to make the love communism of the Christian church impotent. But Jesus' message was decisive, "this world would come to an end"; this eon had had it, and a revolution would take place which would be of a cosmic nature, one which would leave no stone unturned.

The eschatological character of Jesus' preaching is dominant in the New Testament. The whole state, including the temple and everything which presently existed, would be brought down. The Last Judgment would put an end to the present eon. The eschatological character of Mark 13 must be read in relationship to the Sermon on the Mount.

26. Ibid., p. 123.
27. Ibid.

Once the eschatological character of Jesus' ministry is granted, then the moral teachings are credible. The passage about the lilies of the field becomes then not an illustration of Jesus' belief in providence, nor a naive pronouncement about the nature of economic life, but rather the reflection that the new eon is about to break forth and that it is foolish to consider matters of economic stability. When Jesus referred to the two kingdoms, that of God and that of Caesar, he did so out of contempt for the state, anticipating its imminent downfall. The disasters which would destroy the state at the end meant for Jesus a revolution, an entirely new form of social existence which was to come into being.[28] Jesus became the organizer and power behind that new kingdom. He dissolved himself in the community to the same extent as he encompassed it. And Bloch interprets the passage, "I am the vine, ye are the branches," in the light of this identification. The passage from Matthew 25:40, "Inasmuch as ye have done it unto one of the least of these my brethren, ye have done it unto me," is interpreted by Bloch in terms of a love community to which Jesus called his followers. But that community was the prototype for an international community, in which the poor were especially regarded and in which the constituent feature of community was demonstrable concern for the human being. The disciples of Jesus had a social mission to the people at the lowest level of the economic system. Over them there was a "mystical personal authority" in the person of Jesus. Bloch describes the nature of the utopianism of the Bible:

> Christianity is no mere outcry against want; it is an outcry against death and the void, and what it inserts in both of these is the Son of Man.[29]

Bloch translates the concept of the Son of Man into the humanistic concerns of the New Testament utopian community. Although no elaborate social utopianism is worked out in the Bible, its humanistic concerns are always paramount. Jesus came to free man and to enable him to participate in the new exodus, so that he could live in a liberated society (the new kingdom). But nowhere in the New Testament can Bloch find a conception of the kingdom which resembles

28. Ibid., p. 189.
29. Ibid.

that of the "baptized Babylon," or that of the Church. It is St. Augustine who is particularly responsible, Bloch asserts, for initiating the institutionalizing of the utopian community into the Church. According to Bloch, Jesus called for a "leap" not to an inward world, but to a world beyond, to a "fresh start on a new earth." Jesus' dream for a social utopia evolved more and more into the Christian notion of an inward spiritual transformation. The radical renewal of the world which Jesus envisaged became equated with the worldly ambitions of the Church itself.[30]

Bloch points to Joachim di Fiore (A.D. 1200) as the architect of one of the most powerful social utopias known to the Christian world. Joachim did not want to cleanse the Church and the state of their impurities and inequities. He wanted to abolish them in favor of the third kingdom, that kingdom in which the Holy Spirit illumined the minds of all men. Joachim talked about three states in the world: one, in which man is under the law, a second in which man lives by grace, and a third, in which he lives by a broader grace, a future grace. Joachim had, in effect, brought into history the anticipated kingdom, that kingdom which was to come at the end of time. Bloch discovers in Joachim's conception of history that the third stage was to be an "age of monks," that is, of a "universal convent-type consumer communism," in which man was no longer subservient to the law or the state or the Church. The kingdom of the spirit was a this-worldly kingdom, in which Jesus was again the Messiah of a new earth, the king of a liberated democracy in which all men were brothers who formed together a "society of friends." Joachim becomes for Bloch the prototype of revolutionary Christian social utopianism. He set the date for the coming of the communist kingdom on earth. Joachim is the model for the revolution that Jesus envisaged, which the Church destroyed through its political compromises.

Bloch makes the point that the original, revolutionary, utopian character of biblical Christianity, the religion of Jesus, is antithetical to the subsequent ecclesiastical institutionalization of Christendom.

30. Ibid., pp. 126 ff. Bloch does recognize the utopian character of the *civitas Dei* when it is not equated with the Church. "*Socialis vita sanctorum* is a historic-utopian transcendence, because, unlike St. Paul's it is back on earth."(p. 132).

He would agree with Marx on the history of the development of Christian institutionalism:

> The social principles of Christianity have now had eighteen hundred years time to develop. . . . The social principles of Christianity have justified slavery in antiquity, have glorified serfdom in the Middle Ages, and are prepared, if necessary, to defend the oppression of the proletariat, even though with slightly piteous mien. The social principles of Christianity preach the necessity of a ruling class and an oppressed one, and their only pious wish for the latter is that the former may be charitable. The social principles of Christianity raise the Church-bureaucratic compromise of all infamies to heaven, and thereby justify the continuation of those infamies on earth. The social principles of Christianity hold any viciousness committed by the oppressor to be either just punishment for sin original and otherwise, or a trial which the Lord in his wisdom has imposed on the redeemed. The social principles of Christianity preach cowardice, self-contempt, humiliation, humility, submissiveness—in short, all the qualities of scum; and the proletariat that will not be treated as scum has far more need of courage, of self-confidence, of pride, and of a sense of independence than it has of bread. The social principles of Christianity are craven, and the proletariat is revolutionary; so much for the social principles of Christianity.[32]

It is Bloch's extraordinary claim that the authentic biblical witness is to a revolutionary and utopian world view and that the Church is the perverter of Jesus as the original revolutionary!

4. TRANSCENDENCE AS ESCHATOLOGY

Bloch argues that Christianity's deposit to the Western mind is the "principle of hope." He sees a connection between what he conceives of as the origin of all religions as "the dichotomy of man between his present appearance and his non-present essence" and the authentic Christian hope for a new heaven and a new earth. What is more, Bloch believes that Christianity fulfills the demands of the essential characteristics of religion better than any other historical religion. Christianity's messianism and utopianism dramatize more accurately

32. Quoted in ibid., p. 138.

man's situation between "that which is" and "that which can be." It is the Christian's dissatisfaction with the present that gives him hope for the future. It is the Christian's ability to see things from the perspective of the future, of that which man might become, which gives to Western society at once its revolutionary and utopian motifs. But the future for Bloch is unconditionally open ended. He guards against all historical schemes, both Marxist and Christian, which want to fill in the content of that future. The future contains neither an hypostatized God nor an idealized society constructed by the Marxist revolutionary. It is an open future, and its content is to be filled in by the impulses of that radically open future. History is comparable to matter seeking form or to man seeking essence. But it is never ending, and the movement toward the future, prompted by the future itself, can never be absolutely completed. However, hope joins the categories of "real objective possibility" in the historical process. The hopes of mankind have a material and mundane content and are real possibilities in the historical process. But the unconditional character of the future insists upon the unknowability of that content. The socialist transformation of the world and the coming realm of freedom are historical objectives, goals that men dream and scheme about, and historical prognoses can be made about that future. But neither the objective nor the prognosis can be given an absolute character. The future remains radically open, and Bloch will not fill it up with clues to the successive stages of historical development. But his view of the future is essentially optimistic. Hope regains itself in its inconclusiveness: "Even the end of Christ was his beginning."

Bloch's eschatological perspective on history is closely allied to his utopianism. The new is bound up with renewal. He writes:

> The *genuine* reference-and-return is towards what is still in the future, and therefore what has not come to be in the past; ultimately it is a return to the still underived derivation of all that happens.[33]

Novum and *renovatio* are inextricably intertwined. But they are so intertwined in order to give history a futuristic direction:

> There is only one direction in which the seeds of time past tend, the historic modes or forms on the way flourish, and the consolatory

33. Ibid., p. 83.

fantasies of a lost paradise that must be found again seduce. They tend, flourish and seduce only towards a supremely astonishing *fruition*. In that which is new there is only one true form of return: to what was always intended but has never come to be.[34]

It is this conviction that allows Bloch to develop his basic eschatological categories. Man can be loyal in hope, to the hope that a utopia can be created in time. Bloch calls this hope the "eschatology of the present," which for him suggests creative expectation. "*S* is not yet *P*," no subject has its adequate predicate, is another way of saying the same thing: "The history of being itself is the experimental attempt to identify its impulse and origin; the impulse and origin of that history which it is man's task to illumine."[35]

Moses and Jesus were founders of a religion which set itself against the past and its customs and which looked forward to the future. Moses transformed God into the "exodus light of a people" by compelling God to go with him. Jesus posited the utopia of the kingdom of God and called men to participate in it. Both Moses and Jesus introduced the concept of the transcendent, not as an otherworldly spiritual reality, but as the hope that transformed the present and anticipated the future. Or as Bloch puts it, "the more mature the appearance of religions, the more will this specific transcending prove to be that of a most powerful hope, of the totum of a hope that relates the whole world to a whole perfection."[36]

Bloch believes that Jesus' preaching is wholly eschatological in character. Jesus would not give in to the existing "eon": rather he presented a social and economic alternative to it. Jesus' religious movement was thoroughly a social movement at its inception, directed first to the laboring and heavily laden. He gave to them a hope which they could never have known in the midst of their economic oppression. The hope was an impulse that another "eon" would appear in human history, a hope that the oppressive society would be destroyed and the hope of a new era of peace and liberation. Judaism and Christianity thereby posit a "human-eschatological and thus ex-

34. Ibid., p. 84.
35. Ibid., p. 90.
36. Ibid., p. 151.

plosively posited messianism." Bloch proposes a formulation for the religious projection of hope:

> And the farther the subject, with its religious founders, invades and overwhelms the objective mystery of a God conceived as the Supreme Without or the Supreme Above, the more powerfully will man be charged, in an earthly heaven or on a heavenly earth, with the awe of depth and infinity.[37]

But man's awe includes the continued imperative to transform the *humanum.* The numinous character of religion does not exclude the need to effect the radical change in all social relationships that Moses and Jesus called for. In a very particular way, Paul's words in 1 Cor. 2:9 are the classic expression of the utopian expectations of Jews and Christians: "Eye hath not seen, nor ear heard, neither have entered into the heart of man, the things which God hath prepared for them that love him." This is the expression of the historic movement from possibility to actuality, of the historic completion of that which is only posited as a historic possibility. Bloch, following Marx, describes this movement toward utopianism in this way:

> Religion inherited (meta-religion) comes to be the conscience of the last utopian function *in toto:* that function is the self-transcending of man, the transcending in league with the dialectically transcending tendency of man-made history, the transcending without any heavenly transcendence, but with full understanding of that transcendence as a hypostatized anticipation of being-for-itself.[38]

What Bloch means is that the biblical notion of transcendence is that of a future transcendence. It is not a metaphysical or a spatial transcendence but a transcendence in which the historic goal is a redeemed humanity. God appears in man's history as the "hypostatized ideal of the human essence which has not yet come to be." Transcendence is always of what is not yet, the unity of all reality, the kingdom of God, the possibility that utopia can be created here on earth.

37. Ibid., p. 157.
38. Ibid., p. 213.

B. ANALYSIS AND CRITIQUE

Bloch's conception of transcendence as future is instructive to the Jew and Christian. To suggest that "we are not quite there, we are always and deviously on the verge of being there" is a constructive way to introduce movement and a dynamism into a Judaeo-Christian view of history. And then to argue that the future is the transcendent and that transcendence is not an ontological being "up there" is to introduce provocative categories for the Jew and Christian whose God too often seems fixed in some far-off land where angels fear to tread. Bloch's "ontology of the not-yet-being," filled with the categories of possibility for the new and the future, prompt the biblical interpreters to look again to discover what their God is doing. Jürgen Moltmann's *Theology of Hope* could not have been written without Bloch's insight into history as positing a definable and humanistic future. Moltmann can argue, as Bloch has argued before him, that all of Christian theology is eschatological. Eschatology is not one doctrine among many; it is the fundamental one that underlies all of the others and gives to the Christian faith its basically hopeful character. Hope, for the Christian, redeems the present and makes it significant by relating it to a certain future. Hope then becomes the possibility of human and social fulfillment. Transcendence is conceived of in terms of the realization of that fulfillment. Hope opens vistas to man which did not exist before he opened his eyes with the anticipation that the present was being pulled towards the future and that the future was secure. Bloch is accurate in his description of the persistent utopian, nonecclesiastical character of that hope. And Bloch is correct when he argues that it is *The Imitation of Christ* rather than *The City of God* that allows for the social and metaphysical openness necessary for men to cause revolutions and to provoke the energy which creates new kingdoms within the old.

Bloch is a disturber of the peace within Christian ecclesiastical circles. He is an avowed atheist, who denounces the Church because for two thousand years it has attempted to domesticate God. The result is that the transcendent dimension within Christianity has been shockingly shattered. But Bloch comes to the Christian and invites him to look again at the future, that historical future in which there will be (literally) a new heaven and a new earth. He calls upon the Christian to acknowledge that it is his proper function to announce its coming and to enter into alliance with those secular institutions that are striving to bring about its realization.

For Bloch, the future is the only real category of historical thinking. Too often in Christian history it has been only the past because the past assured the veracity of the revelation and provided the institutional framework for its perpetuation. Bloch sees the events that God will bring about in the future more creative for the present than those he achieved in the past. "To hope there belongs the knowledge that in the outside world life is as unfinished as in the Ego that works in that outside world."[39] For the Christian this notion of hope means that the possibility of a meaningful existence rests upon the prior notion that reality itself is in a state of flux and that reality itself has room for new possibilities ahead. Moltmann writes about the unique conception of Christian hope:

> Hence every view which sees the world as a self-contained cosmos, or history as a universal whole that contains and manifests the divine truth, is broken down and transposed into the eschatological key of "not yet."[40]

However, Bloch's view of transcendence as future poses a number of theological problems which ought to be mentioned.

1. BLOCH'S BIBLICAL EXEGESIS

It is highly problematic that one can exegete the Old and New Testaments in the way that Bloch has done, that is, to make them revelatory solely of a utopian messianism. Of course a utopian messianism is present in the Bible, and motifs of revolution and love-communism and a kingdom on earth appear from time to time. But to understand the Old and New Testaments solely in this way is to impose an interpretative formula upon the Bible which destroys the multiplicities of meanings found there. Surely the history of postbiblical Christianity (and Judaism) reveal the diversity of modes of understanding of the content of the Gospel. The history of heresies is instructive of the fact that so-called normative or essential Christianity is difficult to come by. But then if Bloch imposes his own interpretation upon the Gospel, so that the Gospel fits into his revolutionary schema, he cannot claim more than tentative authority for the Bible. Bloch, of course, is not interested in determining which parts of the Bible are authoritative and which are not. However, he is going to the biblical material and eliciting from it a validation for his revolutionary sociopolitical program. If the Bible "brought eschatological conscience into the world" and made the conception of *incipit vita nova* constitutive for a reading of human history, the Bible also brought bishops and priests into an ecclesia, whose master and lord was Jesus Christ himself.

I have no complaint with the appropriation of the eschatological dimension of the Bible for Bloch's own ideological purposes. My anxiety comes about when that eschatological dimension becomes equated with the totality of the content of the Old and New Testaments. Bloch's reading of the Bible is selective but not arbitrary. He imposes upon the biblical witness to God's mighty events in history a highly individualistic notion, a notion which is Bloch's and not the Bible's. The "human-eschatological, hence explosive messianism" is one possible way of conceiving of the revelation of God through Moses to Christ, but it remains only one possible way of conceiving of that revelation. "Aut Christus aut Caesar" is a fundamental New Testament alternative; but there are many other alternatives as well: either God or Satan, goodness or evil, fellowship with Christ or the rejection of Christ, the old age or the new, the spirit or the body, Creation or the Eschaton, among others. Bloch does not come to terms with these alternatives, and hence his biblical exegesis is faulty. But of course, he does not care. He is writing from the perspective of that tradition which has attempted to create utopias on earth, that tradition which has found eloquent expression in the left-wing Christian movements, that of Marcion and Montanus, the Cathari, the Waldenses and the Albigenses, the Hussites, the Anabaptists and the

Illuminati, and the nineteenth century Christian utopians, Tolstoy, Owen, and others. What Bloch has done is to fix attention on the left-wing Christians, the so-called underground Christians, and make that tradition normative for all Christianity. He focuses upon the freedom which shall come to the people of God in the age of the spirit, the age of the disestablished institution, when man shall know God immediately and not through the mediation of institutions. That is his theology of revolution, and it is important for Christian theologians to come to terms with it. But it ought not to be equated with the totality of the Gospel. The Gospel is more complex than that. It contains a multiplicity of meanings and imperatives, and they cannot be comprehended solely in terms of a utopian messianism.

But Bloch is already aware of this fact, because he sets in opposition the revolutionary ethos of Jesus and the institutionalized ecclesiasticism of St. Paul. Such a focus is old hat and sounds much like the liberal nineteenth century theological attempt to discover the "essence" of Christianity in the simple ethical teachings of Jesus without the encrustations of the later bureaucratic and ideological traditions reflected so vividly in St. Paul. The fact is, however, that Jesus is not simply a revolutionary, nor can his ethical teachings be separated from his life and sacrifice on Calvary, in which he "died for the sins of the whole world." Bloch has exploited a biblical image for his own ideological purposes, which he is permitted to do, of course. But the authentic message of the Old and New Testament Gospels have not been affirmed thereby. And the Jewish-Christian understanding of transcendence ought to embrace the totality of the biblical witness and not only a fragment thereof.

2. BLOCH'S ATHEISM

"Only an atheist can be a good Christian," Bloch has written. And he has struggled sincerely with the Jewish-Christian understanding of God and concludes that the mode of God's revelation can only be unknown. Rather than accepting an agnostic position, which might appear to be the natural consequence of this line of reasoning, Bloch wants to be known as an atheist. But he is an atheist in the service of the Gospel. He refuses to posit transcendent metaphysical positions which block the activity of the "Wholly Other" God. By so doing, Bloch suggests the theological tradition of the *via negativa* or the more contemporary dialectical theology, which would define God more by His absence than by His presence. The atheist knows God as the other, as that being which is unlike himself. The atheist knows that God can never be constructed in conceptual terms. Therefore he must be unknown. Therefore it is only wistfulness and profound (ontological) questioning which allows for the possibility of God, but never the necessity of God. Bloch puts it this way (again in his rather oblique fashion):

> If we are in earnest about its transcendent irreality in past and future, the idea of God is fulfilled as an ideal solely by its anthropological dissolution—although by one different, entirely different from the dissolution into existential humanity that has been worked out so far, during the prehistory of mankind. . . . What was intended in the great religions, instead of the many single *hopes,* was *hope itself.* . . . The only truth of the divine ideal is the utopia of the Kingdom, and the premise of that utopia is that no God remains on high, where none is or has ever been anyway.[41]

Bloch is a very special kind of atheist. He is an atheist who destroys all human illusions about God, especially those related to that ecclesiastical tradition which claims to know exactly how God behaves. His atheism allows the inexpressible "Wholly Other" God to be, and Bloch claims no unique ability to know him or any particular mode of correspondence that would unite God and man.

But the question is, then, is Bloch really an atheist, or is he espousing a kind of negative theology that belongs profoundly to the Protestant dialectical theological tradition? Moltmann is sure that his atheism is negative theology.[42] "Only an atheist can be a good Christian," Bloch had written. To which Moltmann responded, "Only a Christian can be a good atheist." But that kind of Teutonic repartee does not impress me in the slightest. If Moltmann discovers in Bloch a substantive ideological framework in which he can place his own "theology of hope," then it is because Bloch is not really an atheist, but a

41. Bloch, *Man on His Own,* p. 216.
42. Ibid., p. 28.

crypto-Judaeo-Christian. And that is my conviction. Bloch does not denounce the God of Abraham, Isaac, and Jacob, who is also the God of Creation and Incarnation. A good atheist ought to do that. Rather he upholds faith in the God of the Old and New Testaments but replaces God language with revisionist Marxist language. In place of the eschatological kingdom, Bloch proposes the Communist utopian society. In place of Christ as the Messiah, Bloch offers the Marxist conception of messianism. In place of the notion of the whole creation groaning and travailing, Bloch suggests the clamor and confusion of a society bent upon its own destruction.

And if my contention is correct, the contention that Bloch is not the virulent atheist that he presents himself to be, then he must be intellectually and politically wedded to Hegelian idealistic categories. Only in this way could Bloch be certain that he could discover the mighty acts of the proletarian revolution in history, and only by so doing could he anticipate the glorious reign of a future humanist society. I do not believe that he can be an atheist in any traditional sense of that term. Either he is ideologically (theologically) a Judaeo-Christian believer, however unorthodox, or he is a Hegelian revisionist. There is no other world view which would allow him to establish the secular *heilsgeschichte* that is filled with such confidence and hope. Why call oneself an atheist when one is not really one? That is a matter that is left unanswered both by Bloch and by Bloch's Christian theological admirers. Bloch is a critic of the Church and a sharp critic of all Jewish and Christian systematic theologies. But that does not make him an atheist. And if his theology of God is a negative theology which affirms the absence of God, then Bloch falls into line with a whole host of normative Christian theologians, including Luther and Tillich.

3. BLOCH'S UTOPIAN MESSIANISM

The Jew and Christian reading Bloch and impressed with his utopian messianism because it introduces again the note of hope into the biblical world view must not be blinded by the fact that no one particular historical development (Marxist communism, however revisionary one may want it to be) can be equated with the eschatological dimension of the Bible. The biblical hope for a new society and the means by which that new society comes into being cannot be equated with the Marxist historical dialectic. This lesson was learned after the historic failures of the Social Gospel to bring about the kingdom of God. Man does not build the kingdom. God alone can bring it into being. Man works to create an environment in history in which man can live as a human being with real concrete indices of what it means to be human. And that is the humanistic and historical counterpart of the doctrine of the Incarnation—to create a world in which there are concrete signs that God has come into that world to redeem it and to make human life more human. But man can never be so sanguine as to believe that he can create a society, either by imaginative social planning or by violent revolution, that can in any way be identified with the eschatological notion of the kingdom of God. That kind of thinking can only lead to a new absolutizing of a particular stage in history with an accompanying secular domestication of God. God becomes identified with one particular epoch in history and thereby loses his historical transcendence. God is involved in history, but as its Lord, not as its dialectical agent. What that means simply is that God can never allow what Bloch wants him to do, that is, to affirm the glorious socialist revolution. That revolution may be the means by which society achieves a historic humanism, but it cannot be identified with what the sovereign God has in mind ultimately for human society.

To say it still another way, Bloch's utopian messianism has enabled Jews and Christians to restore the dimension of hope and the eschatological future which was lost during the period of the great wars. But the biblical world view insists upon the cross as the essential meaning of history. All Christian views of history, therefore, which provide a hopeful perspective on the future must discover that hope about the cross.

As a corollary to the optimism that Bloch engenders about the future, it also ought to be clear that because God is doing something in history, man continues to have a responsibility for that future. Man does not become historically passive because God is affirmed as Lord of history. Man cannot absolutize one historical agent, nor can he give a divine status to one specific political movement. That prohibition assures that God will not be historically domesticated. But man continues to have the obligation to create communities of love where there are only communities of hate. He must be concerned for the poor and the oppressed. He is obliged to deal concretely with material history from a moral and humanistic perspective. Moltmann is close to this point of view in *The Theology of Hope:*

> Does this hope cheat man of the happiness of the present? How could it do so! For it is itself the happiness of the present. It pronounces the poor blessed, receives the weary and heavy laden, the humbled and wronged, the hungry and the dying, because it perceives the parousia of the kingdom for them. Expectation makes life good, for in expectation man can accept his whole present and find joy not only in its joy but also in its sorrow, happiness not only in its happiness but also in its pain. Thus hope goes on its way through the midst of happiness and pain, because in the promise of God it can see a future also for the transient, the dying and the dead. That is why it can be said that living without hope is like no longer living.[43]

4. THE DIVINE AND HUMAN IN BLOCH'S THOUGHT

Bloch champions the Athanasian *homoousios* formula of the unity of Christ's nature with God. What *homoousios* means to Christians is the complete incarnation of God in Christ. What it means to Bloch rather is the complete deification of Christ and man. In *The Principle of Hope* and in *Man on His Own,* he describes the essential truth of religion as the attempt to abolish the hypostasis of the Lord and Master mythologized as Yahweh. "Aut Christus aut Caesar" is the alternative that Bloch finds underlies the being of Yahweh. "And so the good news and its essential content turn atheist with regard to everything that smacks of a power diety."[44] Power is abolished. The God on high is replaced by a new myth, that of the God whose concern is enlightenment and freedom. But that God can never be hypostatized. He is all too human and humane. And religion itself insists upon this reversal of myths so that God might be found in human form. God comes to man not as a transcendent power, but as

43. Moltmann, *Theology of Hope,* p. 32.
44. Ibid., p. 114.

one with man. Christ is God then only as he is man, the man liberated from the tyranny of the myth of the powerful Lord and Master God.

> A paradox then: an increase within religion of the inquiry after its truth; made by existing antitheses to the myth (for it was an alien myth); made so that religion itself can be not opium but protest, central though not dominant: the purposive symbolic expression of a One, a True and a Good without superstition.[45]

Bloch describes the new humanistic *sursum corda* in which man no longer raises his voice to a hypostatized transcendence, but to the good news of salvation: "You will be like God." That is the goal of the humanistic revolution that Bloch champions. *"Eritis sicut Deus"* is the glad tidings of Bloch's gospel.

And then it is clear that Bloch's gospel is a parody of the Christian's, dependent upon it in its essential content, but it is finally a hypostatization of man rather than of God. The Christian's gospel is so much more adequate in its description of the relationship between man and God, affirming the extraordinary claim that the God which the mythologies have hypostatized has chosen to become human himself, to destroy forever all attempts to ascribe power solely to God but to affirm that weakness and suffering also belong to him!

The consequence of the Christian view of Incarnation is much more radical for a liberated humanity than Bloch's revolutionary world view. The Christian looks toward the future with hope, not because of a hope inspired by incipient revolutions, but because of his own conviction that God has already hallowed history by his own presence within history. We are not now dealing with the practical hopes engendered by revolutionary visionaries, but with factual, flesh and blood historical realities. Because Jesus was with us, we know that human life is not only unique but that it is sacred, made holy by the presence of God in history. The Christian's task then is to make real the kind of social environment which is congruent with this fact of Incarnation. The social consequences of such a theological claim may resemble the utopian reconstructionism of Bloch, but they are much more realistic in objective and much more factual in operation. We

45. Ibid.

are to create communities of love, not because of utopian notions that such communities are factually viable, but because God in Christ insists upon them as the foretaste of the new kingdom which will come upon man in the final judgment.

5

TRANSCENDENCE AS SELF-REALIZATION — CARL G. JUNG

A. EXPOSITION

"The world was created imperfect, and God has placed man in it that he may perfect it." So said Paracelsus. The Jungian psychotherapist considers the perfection of man's inner image as the primary task confronting man as he sets about to perfect the world. And it is the psychotherapeutic techniques of Carl Jung (analytical psychology or "complex psychology," as Jung called his own system)[1] that provide the modus operandi by which man can perfect his inner image. Jung's analytical psychology is an empirical approach to "the fields of the psyche." Jung was convinced "that the study of the soul is the science of the future." As a science, it has a purely humanistic objective:

> Psychology is, so to speak, the youngest of the natural sciences and stands at the beginning of its development. It is, though, the science we need most, for it becomes increasingly evident that neither famine, nor earthquakes, nor microbes, nor cancer, but man, is the greatest danger to man, and this for the reason that we have no sufficient protection against psychic epidemics, which can work infinitely more destruction than the greatest catastrophes of nature. It therefore would be in the highest degree desirable to spread under a knowledge of psychology that people could understand from what quarter the greatest danger was threatening them.[2]

1. Jolande Jacobi in one of the prefaces to the Fourth English Edition of *The Psychology of C.G. Jung* (New Haven: Yale University Press, 1943), p. xiv.
2. Ibid., p. xiii.

In this way, the Jungian analysis might have a salutary effect upon the war-ravaged psyches of modern man and may even assist in the creation of new and lasting cultures. When man finds inner peace ("begins to make order in his own soul") or discovers inner perfection, he is no longer subservient to the hysteria of the masses, but he is instead its master. The whole course of human history might therefore be affected. Such is the spirit in which Carl Jung developed his "empirical way" into the field of the psyche.

It is important to recognize the revolutionary character of Jung's thought both because it is a rejection of much of the psychoanalytical discoveries of Jung's own teacher, Sigmund Freud, and also because of the ramifications of that thought for the allied disciplines of metaphysics, theology, aesthetics, and ethics. In a very real way Jung's thought belongs to the realm of the discoverers of that which is radically new. After Jung, all thought is different. No one who thinks can proceed in the traditional way once Jung's concepts have been recognized. Such is the magnitude of Jung's analytical psychology for modern man's self-understanding.[3]

1. THE SCIENCE OF THE SOUL

A fundamental assumption for any real appreciation of Jung's psychology must begin with the acceptance of the full reality of the psyche. For Jung, the psyche is as real as the physical, and although it is not empirically observable as a material phenomenon, it is still fully and unambiguously experienceable.[4] The psyche has its own structures, its own laws, with its own particular mode and means of expression. It is through the psyche that we come to a knowledge of the world and a knowledge of our own being. Jung writes in *Psychology and Religion* that "the psyche is no exception to the general rule that the universe can be established only in as far as our psychic organism permits."[5] The psyche is therefore the medium or agency by

3. Cf. the interpretive studies, Victor White, *God and the Unconscious* (London: Fontana Books, 1952) and Josef Goldbrunner, *Individuation: A Study of the Depth Psychology of Carl G. Jung* (New York: Pantheon, 1955).

4. Jacobi, *Psychology of C. G. Jung*, p. 2.

5. C.G. Jung, *Psychology and Religion* (New Haven: Yale University Press, 1938), p. 49.

which man has any possible understanding of history, culture, science, nature, biology, the world of the saints, as well as an understanding of himself. "Our psychology studies both man in a state of nature and man in a state of culture: therefore it must keep both the biological and the spiritual viewpoints in mind throughout its explanations. As a medical psychology it cannot do otherwise than take man as a whole into consideration."[6] Jung is insistent that his psychotherapy is congruent with modern man's search for spiritual values. He chides the analysts who are followers of Freud and Adler because both of them are "hostile to spiritual values":

> . . . they deal with psychology without the psyche. Theirs are rational methods of treatment which actually *hinder* the realization of meaningful experience. By far the larger number of psychotherapists are disciples of Freud and Adler. This means that the greater number of patients are necessarily alienated from a spiritual standpoint . . . a fact which cannot be a matter of indifference to one who has the realization of spiritual values at heart.[7]

But Jung is ultimately a therapist of the disordered psyche. He attempts to discover the reasons why the psyche becomes disturbed and neurotic, giving a perverted and unhealthy view of man's place in nature and spirit. Jung desires to lead man back from confusion into life. He intends to do that in a very practical way, that is, to help the individual to perfect his inner image, to enable him to come to realistic terms with his self-understanding.

Jung's system is therefore a "practical science" rather than an academic one. To investigate the psyche as the organ with which we are endowed for comprehending the existing universe, to observe its phenomena, to describe them, and to bring them into a meaningful system are his aims and goals. Jung's disciple and faithful interpreter, Jolande Jacobi, writes of Jung's psychotherapeutic system in this way:

> The theological, psychological, historical, physical, and biological standpoints as well as many others are all equally starting points for

6. C.G. Jung, *Psychologie und Erziehung,* quoted in Jacobi, *Psychology of C. G. Jung,* p. 2.

7. C.G. Jung, *Modern Man in Search of a Soul* (New York: Harcourt, Brace & Co., 1933), p. 263.

the investigation of the facts of being; they are interchangeable, even transposable up to a certain point, and they can be utilized at will according to the investigator's problems and special interests. Jung takes the psychological, leaving the others to persóns competent in their fields, drawing however upon his wide acquaintance with psychic reality, so that his theoretical structure is no abstract system created by the speculative intellect but an erection upon the solid ground of experience and resting only upon that.[8]

Jung means by psyche something more than is generally regarded as soul or mind. Psyche is "the totality of all psychological processes, both conscious as well as unconscious."[9] What we call the ego participates in both consciousness and the unconscious and stands somewhere between the two. Consciousness and the unconscious supplement or complement one another. The conscious part of the psyche constitutes but a small part of it and floats, as it were, on the unlimited "sea of the unconscious":

> Under the ego I understand a complex of representations which consti-
> tutes the centrum of my field of consciousness and appears to possess
> a very high degree of continuity and identity.[10]

The ego is also defined as "the subject of consciousness." He defines consciousness as the "function or activity which maintains the relation of psychic contents with the ego." The sphere of consciousness is surrounded by the unconscious, which is filled with a content taken from consciousness. The conscious sphere can deal with only a few contents at one time. The others are repressed because they are disagreeable to consciousness. But they may be raised into consciousness at any time. This is the personal unconscious and contains "forgotten, repressed, subliminally perceived, thought and felt matter of every kind. Suppression, on the other hand, corresponds to a conscious moral decision, while repression represents a rather immoral tendency to rid oneself of unpleasant decisions. Suppression can cause distress, conflict and suffering but it never produces a neurosis. Neurosis is always a substitute for legitimate suffering."[11]

8. Jacobi, *Psychology of C. G. Jung,* p. 3.
9. C.G. Jung, *Psychological Types* (London: Kegan Paul, 1933), p. 588.
10. Ibid., p. 540.
11. Jung, *Psychology and Religion,* pp. 138 ff.

The collective unconscious is distinguished from the personal unconscious because it contains matter, a content, which is not derivative of our own egos but which results "from the inherited possibility of psychical functioning in general, namely from the inherited brain structure."[12] Jacobi quotes Jung on the possibility of a life for the psyche after death:

> We can very well determine with sufficient certainty that an individual consciousness with reference to ourselves has come to an end in death. Whether, however, the continuity of the psychic processes is thereby broken remains doubtful, for we can today assert with much less assurance than fifty years ago that the psyche is chained to the brain.[13]

The collective unconscious unites, or makes possible, the consciousness of every man. It is the "primal datum" out of which individual consciousness is derived.

Human consciousness is built, therefore, upon "the fundamental psychic activity, which consists in the functioning of the unconscious." Children develop from the unconscious state to the conscious. And the development of the human animal reflects the reaction of the individual to general human situations, such as fear, hate, danger, love, power, the relationship between the sexes, between parent and child, to birth and to death, and so forth. The unconscious may have a compensatory function to that of consciousness, drawing upon "general human experience" (and not only individual experience), thereby allowing for an adequate human adjustment of the total psyche.

Jung then develops what he considers to be a law inherent within the structure of the psyche, that is, the relationships of functions constitutionally present in every individual between thought, intuition, feeling, and sensation. In *Psychological Types,* Jung designates a psychological function as "a certain form of psychic energy that remains theoretically the same under varying circumstances and is completely independent of its momentary contents."[14] The point is that all four functions—thought, intuition, feeling, and sensation—

12. Jung, *Psychological Types,* p. 616.
13. Jacobi, *Psychology of C. G. Jung,* p. 11.
14. Jung, *Psychological Types,* p. 547.

are given a priori within the psyche and are not dependent upon any theoretical constructions. There may be no implicit reason why they are found in the human psyche. But they are there. Jung's empirical approach to the study of the psyche assumes that fact: "This conception has shaped itself out of many year's experience." The four functions are mutually exclusive of one another, but together they exhaust all the given possibilities. Furthermore, they symbolize (and mean) completeness (cf. the four arms of the cross, the four points of the compass). The four functions together make up the complete man; however, no man practically has brought to light all that is dark within him. The four functions then remain a theoretical and not a practical possibility.[15]

Thinking is that psychological function which seeks to understand the world and man's place within it in a cognitive way, that is, by an act of thought. It works with the coordinates of truth and falsity. Feeling is the opposite function, for it comprehends the world in a nonconceptual way and makes a judgment on the basis of the gaining of pleasure and the avoidance of pain, on a calculus of that which is agreeable over against that which is disagreeable. Thinking and feeling are mutually exclusive determinants of behavior, although one or the other is predominant in the psyche.

Sensation and intuition are irrational functions according to Jung. Thinking and feeling are rational because of their relationship to correlative evaluations, truth and falsity (thinking) and pleasure and pain (feeling). Both sensation and intuition are perceptions which have neither evaluatory nor interpretive characteristics. Sensation perceives of things as they are. Intuition perceives through its capacity to sense the unconscious "inner perception" of the potentialities in things. Jacobi gives the illustration of the two types confronting a beautiful, blooming spring landscape. The sensation type will see and be aware of the flowers, the trees, color, detail, and so on; the intuitive type will see only the impression the total scene gives.[16] Therefore, intuition and sensation are mutually exclusive functions as are think-

15. Ibid.
16. Jacobi, *Psychology of C. G. Jung,* p. 15; cf. also Jung, *Modern Man in Search of a Soul,* pp. 107 ff.

ing and feeling. But together the four functions allow man to "orient himself in his momentary situation." However, experience demonstrates to Jung that it is usually one of these functions which becomes dominant and which man employs to orient himself to reality. The dominant function becomes the differentiated or superior function; the undifferentiated, the inferior function. The superior function belongs primarily to man's conscious side, the inferior to his unconscious. The two other functions (of the four designated by Jung as constitutive of man's psyche) lie partially in the conscious and partially in the unconscious, thus enabling the individual to make auxiliary use of the other than superior and inferior psychic functions.

With the four psychological functions, Jung has plotted the theoretical structure of the psyche. He can then derive all kinds of symbolic significance from the functions. They represent the duality of light and darkness, male and female, "the universe of opposites." Jung has also discovered that the symbolic representation of opposites is portrayed graphically in the Chinese *Taijitu* symbol, and described so lucidly in *I Ching*. The relationships between the superior and inferior functions and the two less differentiated functions fill the psyche with all sorts of combinations of symbolic representations: the bright regions represent the masculine symbol; the dark, the feminine, the completely unconscious as that of the darkness of the mother's womb. To raise material into consciousness means that the material becomes masculine. Dreams are the medium whereby these functions can be dealt with analytically, that is, therapeutically.

The ideal goal of analysis is to draw upon all four functions in necessary measure: "One can, for example, first comprehend an object cognitively, then track out by means of intuition its inner, concealed potentialities, then touch it all round, as it were, by means of sensation, and finally—if feeling be the inferior function—evaluate it with regard to its agreeableness and disagreeableness."[17] The four functions provide a means by which man orients himself to his world. They provide a kind of "completeness"; they are indispensable to man as he comes to awareness of his world. But his "awareness" takes on the fourfold character: sensation establishes what is actually given (Jung

17. Ibid., p. 20. Cf. also Jung, *Modern Man in Search of a Soul,* p. 107.

is always the empiricist); thinking enables us to recognize the meaning of what is given; feeling informs us of its value; and intuition aids us in the recognition of the variety of possibilities which exist within the given facts. The functional typology is essential for Jung in his analytical technique:

> I would not for anything dispense with this compass on my psychological journey of discovery. . . . I value the type-theory for the objective reason that it offers a system of comparison and orientation which makes possible something that has long been lacking, a critical psychology.[18]

An individual belongs to one of the functional types. But that is a hypothetical judgment because in real life the functional types appear in mixed forms. The inferior function, however, appears to have a modus operandi all its own. Because it is the unconscious, it can break into consciousness indiscriminantly and arbitrarily. In this way, Jung can explain the sometimes completely bizarre and irrational behavior of an individual whose actions customarily are passive and anticipated.

Jung acknowledges, as do his disciples, that the functional typology cannot always provide an exact classification. However, he does pose, as a law of the psyche, the way by which one function stands in a complementary or a corollary relationship to its opposite. But there is always a fundamental polarity between thought-feeling and sensation-intuition; that is, they stand in a complementary or compensatory relationship to one another. Exaggeration of any one function will force the opposite function to assert itself. For example, the overly intellectual individual will find that his feeling side will suddenly and unexpectedly come into consciousness, sometimes in an embarrassing and impulsive manner.

Overdifferentiation of a function (which means something like overemphasis) will lead, at different times in a person's life, to psychic disturbance or mental illness. The persona, according to Jung, is that "function-complex" which relates man to his external world.[19] The

---

18. Jung, *Modern Man in Search of a Soul*, p. 108.
19. C.G. Jung, *Two Essays on Analytical Psychology* (London: Bailliere, Tindall and Cox, 1928), p. 165. "The persona is a function-complex which has come into existence

persona is man's way of coming to grips with the society outside of himself. But it is a compromise, a compromise between the demands of the environment and the constitution of the individual's psyche. The persona, then, can provide a healthy contact with man's environment, but only if the individual is well adjusted to his external and internal worlds. It can also function as a mask behind which the individual can hide his personal inadequacies. The high professionalism of some vocations provides a perfect means by which man can present a certain façade to the world and conceal his enormous inadequacies from his colleagues. Overconcentration upon thought (as in the case of the college professor) perverts the character of the persona and makes subservient the other functions. Psychic disturbance can often result from this situation. And what is more, the contacts these people make with the external world are oftentimes stereotyped and inauthentic.

The collective consciousness plays a role in the behavior of the individual. By the collective consciousness Jung means something similar to what Freud meant by the superego, "the totality of the traditions, conventions, rules, prejudices, and norms in a human collective that are followed consciously but unreflectively by the individual." But in addition to the collective consciousness of society, which causes individuals to act in inflated ways because of titles and social expectations, there is also the "collective unconscious" of the individual psyche, that deep, underlying layer of psychic energy which can cause the individual to be swallowed up by his interior world. The persona, therefore, is dependent both upon the external world (human society) and the internal world. Any maladjustment of either necessarily leads to an imbalance in the persona and a consequent psychic problem or disturbance.

Jung develops other ways by which to evaluate the type of psychological character of an individual. Creative persons, artists for example, are constitutionally closer to their unconscious and, therefore, cannot easily be typed. Artistic creativity means for Jung that the

---

for reasons of adaptation or necessary convenience, but by no means is it identical with the individuality. The function-complex of the persona is exclusively concerned with the relation to the object." Quoted in Jacobi, *Psychology of C. G. Jung*, p. 24.

collective symbols of humanity, which rest in man's unconscious, are activated in the finished work of art: "Who, however, speaks in primordial images speaks as with a thousand tongues, he grips and overpowers, and at the same time he elevates that which he treats out of the individual and transitory into the sphere of the eternal. . . ."[20] Jung recognizes two differing types, or attitudes, which depend upon the manner by which the individual comes into contact with his world. One is extroversion; the other, introversion. These are what Jung calls the "reaction habitus": "the central switchboard from which on the one hand external behavior is regulated and on the other specific experiences are formed."[21] Introversion and extroversion are "typical attitudes" of man, "essential bases" which condition the whole psychic process and determine the "style" of behavior and the nature of subjective experience. Jung formulates the distinction between introversion and extroversion in the following way:

> There is a whole class of men who at the moment of reaction to a given situation at first draw back a little as if with an unvoiced "No," and only after that are able to react; and there is another class who, in the same situation, come forward with an immediate reaction, apparently confident that their behavior is obviously right. The former class would therefore be characterized by a certain negative relation to the object, and the latter by a positive one.[22]

The introverted person's reactions are determined by subjective factors; the extroverted by the external, socially valid norms. The extrovert orients himself primarily by what lies outside of himself; the introvert does not make the same kind of external adjustment to the world. He begins to confront his world with his own subject, the objective world taking a place of secondary significance.

Extroversion and introversion are attitudinal types and as such are much more closely related to biological factors (for example, one's constitution, development from puberty to adolescence). And it is because of this fact that it is more difficult to effect a change from one

20. C. G. Jung, *Contribution to Analytical Psychology* (London: Kegan Paul, 1928), p. 248. Quoted in Jacobi, *Psychology of C. G. Jung,* p. 35.

21. Jung, *Modern Man in Search of a Soul,* p. 99.

22. Ibid., p. 98.

attitudinal type to another. There is also a complementary relationship between the two. When consciousness is extroverted, the unconscious is introverted, and vice versa. And when the opposite, unconscious attitude breaks through, the consequences are disastrous for the individual personality. The extrovert can become intensely egocentric with the interior world determining his behavior; and conversely, the introvert can become a maladjusted extrovert. In addition, the introversion-extroversion attitudes, with their compensatory unconscious opposites, can come into conflict with individuals who possess the same complex of conscious and unconscious factors—with the result that one person projects upon another his own conscious (and unconscious) attitudes. The consequence is, of course, sheer havoc for any kind of so-called normal human relationships.

Other problems that Jung recognizes as a consequence of his psychological typology are the following:

Chronological dysfunctionality, or the changing psychological situation after the person has reached forty, with a concomitant realignment of conscious and unconscious factors.

Immature psychological functions, in which one of the four functions is well developed. The child's personality ought to change and mature by the end of adolescence. If it does not, the result is an infantile personality in an adult's body. A too slight development of the functions is as detrimental as a one-sidedly overdifferentiated one.

Anachronistic psychological functionality, that is, the situation of the individual who is extroverted in youth, that time when he can best come to know his world in an externalized way, but remains extroverted in later life, or that time when he ought to begin to draw in upon himself and "find his way home."

One-sided orientation to life, an overexaggeration upon the thinking function to the exclusion of feeling. No feeling is, or can be, present in man's relationship to his fellow men. Neurosis and psychic disturbance always result but are brought about because the functions and the attitudes demand unity in equal proportions both in consciousness and in practice.

Jung's typology gives us the following (combining the functions with the attitudinal types):

1. the extroverted thinking type
2. the introverted thinking type
3. the extroverted feeling type
4. the introverted feeling type
5. the extroverted sensation type
6. the introverted sensation type
7. the extroverted intuition type
8. the introverted intuition type

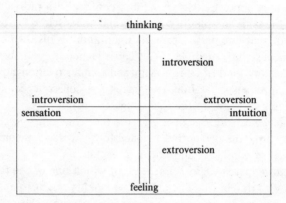

The unconscious has a complex character and is constructed of both personal and collective psychic factors. Jacobi describes the unconscious in this way:

1. Memories
2. Repressed material ⟩ Personal unconscious
3. Emotions and primitive drives
4. Eruptions from the deepest part of the unconscious ⟩ Collective
5. That part of the consciousness that can never be made / unconscious
   conscious[23]

As one descends the different levels of the unconscious one loses control increasingly over its expression and its differentiation. But the unconscious works in relation to consciousness. Therefore, as consciousness works to adjust itself to reality in a direct and purposive

23. Jacobi, *Psychology of C.G. Jung,* p. 40.

way, the unconscious work also effects an adjustment, but to an internal standard. In this way, a maladjusted consciousness can be restored to balance and the individual can be restored to psychic health.

The unconscious is brought to consciousness by means of symptoms, complexes, dreams, and mythological symbols (or archetypes).

Symptoms: Jung defines symptoms as the phenomenon of the obstruction of the normal flow of energy, which can be manifested psychically or physically. There is an inadequate adjustment within consciousness and a widening of consciousness ought to take place.

Complexes: Jung defines them as "psychological parts split off from the personality, groups of psychic contents isolated from consciousness, functioning arbitrarily and autonomously, leading thus a life of their own in the dark sphere of the unconscious where they can at any moment hinder or further conscious acts."[24] Jung speaks of the "nuclear element" as the primary meaning of the complex. This is almost completely unconscious and is thereby beyond the control of the individual. "The nuclear element has a constellating power corresponding to its energetic value."[25] The nuclear element is a center of functional disturbance and can, in situations of stress, both internal and external, bring the whole state of psychic equilibrium under its control. The individual can find himself determined by "foreign," unconscious factors, which bring the whole state of consciousness under their perverse control.

The complex behaves autonomously because it resists the intentions of consciousness. As Jung describes complexes in *Modern Man in Search of a Soul,* "[they] come and go as they please." That is to say that the complex is a psychic content outside of the control of the conscious mind. It leads a separate existence and preys upon the intentions of consciousness. But the primary point is that the complex acts as a foreign body in the field of consciousness. The complex can also appear as a conflict of a sexual, moral, social, or other nature. And everyone is subject to complexes. Jung acknowledges this fact and has learned well the lesson of Freud's *Psychopathology of Every-*

24. Jung, *Modern Man in Search of a Soul,* p. 90.
25. Jung, *Contributions to Analytical Psychology,* p. 11.

day Life. A complex indicates, so Jung says, "the unresolved problems of the individual, the points at which he has suffered a defeat . . . and where there is something he cannot evade or overcome—his weak spots in every sense of the word."[26] The complex points to the "unfinished" (in the sense of the requirement of adaptation and the individual's constitutional inability to meet the challenge) in the individual and represents the inability of the individual to accept the whole of his unique and individual nature.

Dreams: These provide the most effective means through which one might know the content of the unconscious. The dream cannot be dealt with in terms of causality. It also defies comprehension in terms of time and space. Its language is also difficult for comprehension. It is, Jung says, symbolic and prelogical. It requires, therefore, special means for interpretation. The dream allows the easiest access to the contents of the unconscious. For "the problem of dream analysis stands and falls with the hypothesis of the unconscious; without this the dream is a senseless conglomerate of crumbled fragments from the current day."[27] Dreams are also revelatory of personal conflicts and, in many instances, manifestations of the collective unconscious.

Jung describes the analysis of the dream in this way:

> The dream cannot be explained with a psychology taken from consciousness. It is a determinate functioning, independent of will and wish, of intention and conscious choice of goal. It is an unintentional happening, as everything in nature happens . . . it is on the whole probable that we continually dream, but consciousness makes while waking such a noise that we do not hear it. If we could succeed in keeping a continuous record we should see that the whole follows a definite trend.[28]

This implies that the dream is a natural psychic phenomenon with an autonomy peculiar to the unconscious.

The dream is a direct experience of the unconscious and is the means by which the unconscious exhibits regulative activity. "The dream gives a true picture of the subjective state, while the conscious mind denies that the state exists, or recognizes it only grudgingly. It

26. Ibid., p. 91.
27. Ibid., p. 2.
28. C.G. Jung, *Seminar on Children's Dreams,* quoted in Jacobi, *Psychology of C. G. Jung,* pp. 94–95.

presents the subjective state as it really is. It has no respect for my conjecture or for the patient's view as to how things should be, but simply tells how the matter stands. I have therefore made it a rule to put dreams on a plane with psychological fact."[29] The dream is a pure manifestation of the psyche, of the unconscious primal nature that Jung calls the objective psychic. The dream then reveals the internal functioning of the unconscious as that unconsciousness is indifferent to the conscious attempt of the ego to adjust itself to the outer world. The purpose of unconsciousness is "the maintenance of the continuity of the psychic processes." As such it protects the self from overexaggeration of any one of the psychic functions, but its objective is always related to its own life, to the completion of the psyche. Jung uses the term compensation to mean the totality at which the unconscious psyche aims and which the dream expresses. The psyche has this compensation function as a constitutionally given ("congenitally given") datum of its nature. For Jung,

> the psyche is a self-regulating system that maintains itself in equilibrium as the body does. Every process that goes too far immediately and inevitably calls forth a compensatory activity. Compensation, then, becomes a *law* of psychic happening. And it is the same for the relationship between consciousness and the unconscious. It is always helpful, when we set out to interpret a dream to ask: What conscious attitude does it compensate?[30]

But the dream does not conform to a normative standard of "dream meanings." Jung is too much the empiricist, and at heart a vigorous humanist, to allow for standardized and formalized interpretations of dreams. The context of the dreamer must be considered, as well as the individual and social problems involving the individual. Jung also asks that we take into account the dreamer's philosophical, religious, and moral convictions. The dream symbol does not have a fixed character but is a symbol of something not yet consciously recognized or conceptually formulated. But other dreams express common psychic material which belongs to the corporate consciousness of the race.

Fantasies and visions are also revelatory of the content of the

29. Ibid., p. 6.
30. Ibid., p. 20.

unconscious. Their content is derivative of the personal or collective unconscious and is similar to the materials of dream analysis.

Archetypes: These are unconscious themes of a symbolic and mythological nature, revealing materials which belong properly to universal world history. But they are presented in dreams in a symbolic way. "The dream speaks in images, and gives expression to instincts, that are derived from the most primitive levels of nature."[31] The archetype "represents or personifies certain instinctive premises in the dark, primitive psyche, in the real but invisible roots of consciousness."[32] The archetype gives expression to an instinct, a psychologically necessary way of responding to a given situation. The behavior engendered by the instinct often may appear irrational. But the behavior is determined in an almost biological way and means that the individual has inherited certain ways of functioning psychologically. Jung again speaks of the archetype as a "law" of the unconscious psyche. But the law is an inherited one and gives to the individual a subjective potentiality to experience in a certain way. Man could have no experiences at all if he were not born with a subjective potentiality to experience parents, a wife, children, birth, death, community, professional life, and God. Man is born with an a priori form of the world into which he is born.

But there is also another side to the archetype, that of its numinous character, its imperceptibility and inaccessibility. It exercises its function in the subjective realm of the soul. What this means practically is that although we can control the content of our consciousness to some degree, the unconscious is beyond our control and has a life of its own. The archetype forms the centers of consciousness and its fields of force. Jacobi comments:

> According to these forces contents sinking into the unconscious are subjected to a new, *imperceptible order,* inaccessible to conscious cognition, are often bent in their course and altered in their appearance and meaning in a manner incomprehensible to us. It is this absolute inner order of the unconscious that forms our refuge and help in the acci-

31. Ibid., p. 30.
32. C. G. Jung and C. Kerenyi, *Essays on a Science of Mythology* (London: Routledge and Kegan Paul, 1950), p. 110.

dents and commotions of life, if we only understand how to "get in touch" with it. So it becomes comprehensible that the archetype can alter our conscious adjustment or even transform it into its converse.[33]

The archetype functions then as an aid to a proper conscious response to a situation. It works according to a life and logic of its own; and it is the unconscious telling consciousness what ought to be an adequate and healthy response.

Jung describes the archetypes as "psychic organs," and what he means by that is that archetypes belong inherently to consciousness. They are "objectifications and concretizations belonging to consciousness."[34] They belong to the realm of light, apart from earthly reality, but they also belong to the realm of darkness; they are bipolar, or they circumscribe reality, as Jung puts it. But the archetype is preexistent and immanent within the psyche, functioning as a kind of axial system upon which the experiences of the human being gather. The "images" which are produced by experience are already present within the psyche in a fundamental and primordial sense. Jung uses the image of a crystal formation:

> The form of these archetypes is perhaps comparable to the axial system of a crystal, which predetermines as it were the crystalline formation in the saturated solution, without itself possessing a material existence. This existence first manifests itself in the way the ions and then the molecules arrange themselves. . . . The axial system determines, accordingly, merely the stereometric structure, not, however the concrete form of the individual crystal . . . and just so the archetype possesses . . . an invariable core of meaning that determines its manner of appearing always only in principle, never concretely.[35]

The archetype is present in a general sense within the whole human species. As it raises itself into consciousness, it brings with it a storehouse of images and symbols. And these images and symbols are related to human self-understanding. The archetype is a picture of the primal patterns of human behavior; it is a "self-portrait of the instinct." It is for Jung an "eternal presence," and the fundamental

33. Jacobi, *Psychology of C. G. Jung*, p. 54.
34. C.G. Jung, "Der Geist der Psychologie," *Eranos-Jahrbuch 1946* (Zürich: Rhein Verlag, 1947).
35. C.G. Jung, *Eranos-Jahrbuch 1938*, p. 410.

problem for psychology is whether consciousness perceives it or not. It has the capacity to appear on different levels of the psyche and in a complexity of forms. But it remains the same in its basic structure and meaning. When it is ill defined and poorly developed, it can be said to be found in the deepest level of the collective unconscious. Here the archetypes appear in the form of "axial systems," without specific content, but prior to individual experience. When experience is immediate and intensely personal, the archetype through which the experience is expressed will be defined in a complicated but well-detailed manner, the material which the archetype represents will be general and impersonal, and the language employed will be vague and elementary; "such an archetype in its poverty and simplicity neverthe-less contains potentially all the manifoldness and richness of the living universe." Jung conceives of the archetype as participating in the drama of the human race:

> All mythicized natural processes are symbolical expressions of the inner and unconscious drama of the soul which human consciousness is able to grasp by the way of projection, that is, reflected in natural events. Unconscious man finds in all the processes of nature analogies to the drama that takes place in the acting and suffering subject.[36]

Myths are therefore the language of the archetype and, as such, illustrate the whole history of mankind.

> The archetypes correspond to the truths of life. The unconscious has experienced the life of the individual, of families, tribes and nations innumerable times and possesses a most vital and inward feeling of the rhythm of growth, flowering and dying.[37]

The image of "mother" is often used by Jung as illustrative of the way by which the archetype functions in the psyche. Mother is a preexistent structural form, prior to every empirical manifestation of the motherly. It represents all of the human (conscious) and symbolic (unconscious) forms that the motherly is capable of taking. According

36. C.G. Jung, "Über die Archetypen des kollektiven Unbewussten," in *The Integration of Personality*, translated by Stanley Dell (New York: Farrar & Rinehart, 1940).
37. C.G. Jung, from *Wirklichkeit der Seele*, p. 19. Quoted in Josef Goldbrunner, *Individuation* (New York: Pantheon, 1955), p. 108.

to Jung, the "great mother" archetype is the same in the soul of present-day man as it was in mythological times. "Becoming conscious," as a phenomenon of modern man, has to do with the distinction between the ego and the mother. Jacobi explains:

> Gaining consciousness, formulating ideas—that is the father-principle of the Logos, which in endless struggle extricates itself ever and again from the mother's womb, from the realm of the unconscious. In the beginning both were one, and one can never be without the other, as light in a world where it was uncontrasted with darkness would lose its meaning.[38]

The world is made up of these archetypal opposites. Without them, according to Jung, the world could not exist.

The language expressed by the archetype in the unconscious is a picture language, or symbol language. But it is not a literal language and therefore cannot be translated completely into an intelligible language.

> What an archetypal content is always expressing is first and foremost a figure of speech. If it speaks of the sun and identifies with it the lion, the king, the hoard of gold guarded by the dragon, or the force that makes for the life and health of man, it is neither the one thing nor the other, but the unknown third thing that finds more or less adequate expression in these similes, yet—to the perpetual vexation of the intellect—remains unknown and not to be fitted into a formula.[39]

Archetypes are related directly to the "possibilities of fundamental human experiences," and therefore their number is limited. They are primordial in character and represent a "primal experience," which experience man has had since the beginning of time. And they are the same in all cultures, represented in mythologies, fairy tales, mysteries, and religious traditions. Illustrations of the archetype are the night sea voyage, the wandering hero, the sea monster, the setting and rebirth of the sun, the exploits of Prometheus and Hercules, the myths of creation, the fall from paradise, the virgin birth of the deity, the

---

38. Jacobi, *Psychology of C. G. Jung*, p. 61.

39. C. G. Jung and C. Kerenyi, *Essays on a Science of Mythology*, Bollingen Series xxii (New York: Pantheon Books, 1949), pp. 105 ff.

betrayal of the hero, the dismembering of Osiris, and so forth; also, the peasant, the craftsman, the saint, the visionary, the ecstatic, the warrior, hero, priest, Don Juan, the prostitute, the simpleton, the satanic man, the contemplative, the activist. "It is perhaps surprising," Jung writes, "but if one surveys an adequate variety of ethnological facts, one begins to see that these types occur throughout the human world." The forms of the snake, the fish, the sphinx, the world tree, the great mother, the enchanted prince, the journey of the magi, the wise man, paradise, and so on represent certain contents of the collective unconscious. The archetype is capable of coming to life in the individual psyche and, as it were, "recapitulating" the great mythologies that have been transmitted to men through the centuries. The archetype for Jung represents a storehouse of latent and potential knowledge of man's relationship to God, the neighbor, and the world: "To open this store to one's own psyche, to wake it to new life and to integrate it with consciousness means therefore nothing less than to take the individual out of his isolation and to incorporate him in the eternal cosmic process."[40]

The archetype has an autonomous power that forces its way into the health-producing effects of the life of the psyche. Archetypes have always functioned as the bearers of salvation, and not recognizing them has led to serious and deleterious consequences in the soul. But it is the major religions of man that have been the bearers of the archetypes into the present, in their potential form, to heal and restore health. Dogma and institutionalization pervert their primal effectiveness and their magic powers. But they are still alive, in the dark recesses of the psyche, waiting to find the avenues of possible expression, to provide wholeness and light and wonder and life to man.

In actual analysis, Jung discovered that symbol interpretation often led the analyst to the archetype. The symbol is for Jung a "libidinal parable" because it functions in such a way as to express the dynamics of the mind in pictorial ways. The symbol is therefore an incarnation of psychic material.

40. Jacobi, *Psychology of C. G. Jung*, p. 64.

2. TRANSCENDENCE AS THE WAY OF INDIVIDUATION (SELF-REALIZATION)

Jung's analytical psychology must be conceived of in terms of its objective of healing or salvation *(Heilsweg)*. It intends to bring the individual to a state of wholeness, of psychic health, of knowledge and perfection of his personality, and it intends to do so in a practical way, encouraging the individual to find the means of his own healing. Wholeness of personality is attained when the two parts of the psyche, the conscious and the unconscious, are joined together and stand in a living relation to one another. That then is the ideal of Jungian psychotherapy. The analyst plays an important role in the healing process, but only as he (the analyst) is willing to actually live with the difficulties of the other person. The Jungian maxim is simply that "the psychotherapist can bring those whom he leads only so far as he himself has come," which implies an active, dialectical relationship with the patient.

But psychic wholeness is always a relative notion, a realization of man's being which is an objective to be grasped during the entire life of man. "The personality as a full realization of the wholeness of our being is an unattainable ideal. Unattainability is, however, never anything against an ideal; for ideals are nothing but signposts, never goals."[41] The full realization of personality can never become a historical actuality because the unconscious can never be made completely conscious and because the unconscious contains the greater amount of energy. Jung's impossible ideal brings with it the potentialities for man to become truly human. It means that man stands aloof from the "undifferentiatedness and unconsciousness of the herd"; it means that man accepts the call of destiny found deep within his own unconscious. "Only he who can deliberately say 'Yes' to the power of the destiny he finds within himself becomes a personality."[42] Only then does he possess the ability to become part of a community, "to be an integral part of a group of human beings and not merely a cipher in

41. C. G. Jung, *Integration of the Personality* (New York: Farrar and Rinehart, 1939), p. 287.
42. Ibid., p. 296.

the mass, which always consists only of a sum of people and never can become, like the community, a living organism that receives life and bestows life."[43]

The realization of oneself, in both the ideal sense and the realistic sense, in both an individual sense and a collective sense, is what Jung terms the way of individuation: "Becoming an individual being and, in so far as we understand by individuality our innermost, final, incomparable uniqueness, becoming one's own Self."[44] Jung establishes as the objective of wholeness man's recognition of his uniqueness in relationship to his collective responsibilities but also his recognition of his uniqueness in its place within the whole.

The process of individuation is an intense analytical effort. Jung describes it as the approach of the personality toward a psychic totality. It brings one ultimately to recognize oneself for what one by nature really is and not what one would like to be. And this process recognizes the scientific character of the unconscious elements in the psychic development of personality. Jacobi describes the process as follows:

> [It] concentrates, with strictest integrity and under the direction of consciousness, upon the internal psychological process, eases the tension in the pairs of opposites by means of highest activation of the contents of the unconscious, acquires a working knowledge of their structure, and leads through all the distresses of a psyche that has lost its equilibrium, hacking through layer upon layer, to that center which is the source and ultimate ground of our psychic existence—to the inner core, the Self.[45]

The way of individuation (or the objective of self-realization) is the highest task that man can set for himself. For oneself it means that one anchors oneself in the eternal and indestructible, in the primal nature of the objective psyche. The individual places himself, Jung says, in the eternal stream, in which birth and death are only stages on life's way and in which the isolated ego is no longer the sum total of life's meaning. Man is related in a new way to his fellow man, in

43. Jacobi, *Psychology of C. G. Jung,* p. 140.
44. C. G. Jung, *Two Essays on Analytical Psychology* (London: Bailliere, 1928), p. 183.
45. Jacobi, *Psychology of C. G. Jung,* p. 141.

a way of kindness and compassion because he himself has experienced the darkest side of life. He is related differently to the collective, too, because he can present to the collective an individual who is maturely responsible to the obligations assigned to him by his place in society. Jung's analytical objective is the whole person, the person who can stand in responsible relationship to both an individual consciousness and to the collective.

The way of individuation has been carefully plotted by Jung. The archetypal symbols determine the direction of the process.

The first stage of the process leads to the experience of the shadow, which is the archetypal figure of the "other aspect" of the personality. Man may meet his shadow side in a number of ways; he may meet it when his functional and attitudinal type are made conscious, that is, when he has differentiated only his principal function and attempts to apprehend inner and outer realities solely with this organ of experience. The other three sides of his psyche therefore must remain in the dark and must be extracted from it piece by piece so that they too may live. Or one may encounter the shadow in an inner symbolic figure, in a dream representing one or several of the dreamer's mental traits in personified form; or it can represent an outer figure, someone taken directly from one's own environment. But the shadow may also be a positive figure and may be the personification of the content of the psyche that has not been lived or has been excluded or repressed during one's life. Or it may personify the tendency in every man to that which is inferior, primitive, unadapted, awkward, and dark. The shadow bars the way to the creative depths of the unconscious with the dark mass of that stuff of experience we have never admitted into our life.[46]

To confront one's shadow is to come to terms with one's own nature. We accept the fact that the darkness is indeed within us.

The second stage of the process of individuation is characterized by the encounter with what Jung calls the "soul-image." It is the meeting of the anima with the animus, the meeting of the image of the other sex that we carry in us, both as individuals and as representatives of a species. Jung argues that we experience the elements of the opposite

46. Jung, *Psychology and Religion,* quoted in Jacobi, *Psychology of C. G. Jung,* p. 148.

sex that are always present in one's own psyche: "Every man carries his own Eve in himself." And Jung elevates that proposition to the status of psychic law; and the soul-image is a firmly constituted functional complex: everything which is latent and unexperienced and undifferentiated in the psyche (man's Eve and woman's Adam) is always projected into experience. That means that the individual relates to another who represents the qualities of one's own soul. Or if the projection is an inner one, dreams, fantasies, even visions, these can give expression to a "whole sheaf of contrasexual traits of our psyche." The mother is the first bearer of the soul-image; later it is those women who excite the man, whether positively or negatively.

The soul-image coincides with the psychic function that is the least clarified in the unconscious; for this reason, its character will always be diametrically opposed to the most differentiated function and will be symbolized by a corresponding specific figure. For example, the anima of the scholar will be characterized by a primitive emotional romanticism; the intuitive, by the earthy and realistic type of woman.[47] Jung affirms that when one has seen the contrasexual function within one's own psyche, then he has his emotions under control. But again and again Jung assures his readers that such a recognition is an achievement of maturity. "The meeting with the soul-image regularly signifies that the first half of life with its necessary adjustment to outer reality and the thereby conditioned direction of consciousness outward is ended, and now the most important step in inward adjustment, the confrontation with one's own contrasexual component, must begin."[48] Jungian analysis attempts to make conscious the soul-image so that man may have adequate knowledge of the contrasexual in his psyche.

The third stage is the appearance of the archetype of the old wise man, the personification of the spiritual principle within man; the corresponding material principle is within woman—the *magna mater,* or the great earth mother. Jung believes that we can get back to the essence of man, that is, to the primordial image of an essential human nature. Man is characterized as principally spiritual in his essential

47. Jacobi, *Psychology of C. G. Jung,* pp. 159–160.
48. Ibid., p. 162.

nature. The individual is truly free only when he begins to recognize his own true individuality; "for the man the second and true liberation from the father, for the woman that from the mother, and therewith the first perception of their own unique individuality."[49]

The self is the archetypal image that represents the union of both the conscious and the unconscious. "The self is not only the mid-point but also the circumference, taking in consciousness and the unconscious; it is the center of the psychic totality, as the ego is the center of consciousness."[50] It is the last stage on Jung's way of individuation, it is what Jung calls self-realization. When man reaches this point, then he may be considered a whole man. Man has then integrated his inner and outer selves into one basic reality. Life for man is completely transformed. He recognizes the impulses which have come from his unconscious. He has made them conscious and has acknowledged and recognized their reality. "One must stay with it," writes Jung, "and the process begun by self-observation must be lived through in all its developments and joined on to consciousness with as much understanding as possible. This naturally often implies an almost unbearable tension because of the unparalleled incommensurability between conscious life and the process in the unconscious which latter can be experienced only in one's inmost feelings and may nowhere touch the visible surface of life."[51] But the individual personality is never without its conflicts. Suffering pertains to life. One must never attempt to escape from conflicts in a false or artificial way. To do so leads inevitably to psychic disease. Suffering which results from a genuine experience, Jung writes in *Psychology and Religion,* always carries with it the feeling of a significance, later to be realized, and of a spiritual enrichment.[52]

Jung describes the nature of that personality which has effected self-realization in this fashion:

> The more one becomes conscious of oneself through self-knowledge and corresponding action, the more that layer of the personal overlay-

49. Jung, *Two Essays on Analytical Psychology,* p. 262.
50. Jung, *Integration of the Personality,* p. 96.
51. Ibid., p. 153.
52. Jung, *Psychology and Religion,* pp. 91–92.

ing the collective unconscious vanishes. Thence arises a consciousness no longer captive in a petty and personally sensitive ego-world but participant in a wider, in the world of objects. This broader and deeper consciousness is also no more that sensitive, egoistic bundle of personal ambitions, wishes, fears, and hopes that must be compensated or perhaps corrected by unconscious personal tendencies, but it is a function of reference connected with the object, the outer world, placing the individual in unconditional, binding, and indissoluble community with it.[53]

The self, Jung continues, "is strange to us and yet so near, quite our own and yet unknowable, a virtual mid-point of mysterious nature. . . . The beginnings of our whole psychic life seem to be inextricably in this point, and all our loftiest, ultimate aims tend thither."[54] The self is the point in time and space about which our psychic life revolves; it is at the same time the goal of our conscious and unconscious lives. The self, therefore, can be psychologically justified but never scientifically verifiable. It is a transcendental postulate akin to Kant's *Ding an sich.* It represents that in the psyche which is unfathomable but also the indispensable presupposition for the conscious life of man. The self can also function as an ethical objective in terms of the goal of self-realization. One can also speak about it in religious terms as the image of God in man, the "divine spark," the "central fire." It may be likened to the Christian ideal of the kingdom of God within man. The self, according to Jung, is that point within the human being where God's likeness to man can be recognized most distinctly.

The way of individuation is a way of self-knowledge and self-control in a prospective sense. It intends the construction of a psychic totality within the individual which is entirely new and which attempts to restore the individual's faith in God or in himself or in the meaningful and purposeful quality of life. It is Jung's attempt to confront the serious disorientation of modern life by projecting the goal of the totality and unity of all of life, including the conscious and the unconscious sides of man's being. The way of individuation is a spiritual act, an act of illumination; it confers a new spirit on man, which Jung likens to the Christian rite of baptism. Individuation

53. Jung, *Two Essays on Analytical Psychology,* p. 189.
54. Ibid., p. 265.

makes man a transcendental being, a superior man, *anima naturalites christiana,* the man who realizes the Christ symbol within himself. Self-realization creates a new *Weltanschauung,* a new picture of the world within which man lives. His consciousness is heightened as he becomes aware of the new world in which he lives. Life takes on a completely new meaning. The problems of the world before which man stands can now be dealt with in a proper way. They remain insoluble, but man need not be devastated by them. The problems cannot be solved; but they can be transcended. The self-realized personality is that personality which has the capacity to grapple with the basic problems of life. Because his consciousness has been raised, a broader horizon comes into view. The problems lose their urgency. Man does not panic because of them. The reality of the storm is not diminished, but the individual possesses the internal strength to rise above the storm.

The archetypal symbol of man's transcendent power is the unifying symbol, which represents all of the partial systems of the psyche integrated into the self upon a transcendentally higher plane. The unifying symbol represents the resolution of opposites, the *coincidentia oppositorum,* the unification of the different pairs of opposites in the psyche into a higher synthesis. It is, however, not a metaphysical transcendence but a functional transcendence, in which the personality has been transformed. At that point, the process of individuation reaches its end. Equilibrium has been reached between the ego and the unconscious. The symbolic representation is often in the form of a magic circle or a mandala or a center of totality.

B. ANALYSIS AND CRITIQUE

Jung's analytical psychology appears in the guise of a cryptotheology. Jung interprets the experience of the self and the realization of the self in terms which are religious and theological. The experience of the self is similar to the experience of God. The goal of individuation enables man to experience the Godlike or Christlike quality within himself. Christ becomes for Jung the archetypal symbol for the full integration of personality. But God and Christ are, for Jung, found within the soul. Jung is fond of quoting Meister Eckhardt: "God must for ever be born in the soul." God will appear in man by means of the process of individuation. "We must direct our patients to the place where the One, the All-Uniting arises in them," Jung affirms. Redemption becomes for Jung a spiritual journey in which the self comes to terms with itself and with the world outside of itself.

Jung's system is therefore attractive and immediately appealing to all practitioners of the "cure of souls." He awakens within man the need to find again the meaning of life, meaning which for many of Jung's patients can only be gotten from the historic Western religions of Judaism and Christianity. Jung criticizes the rigidity of dogma and ecclesiastical institutionalism but not the spiritual deliverance and freedom that Judaism and Christianity hold out as moral and spiritual objectives for man.

However, I want to maintain that the attraction of Jung's system to the Judaeo-Christian is of dubious value. It does not lead to an intellectual nor a psychological nor a spiritual strengthening of the Jewish-Christian theological position, but rather to its diffusion and ultimate dissolution.

1. THE HOLISTIC FALLACY

One can begin a criticism of Jung with the assertion that he commits in the grossest way imaginable the holistic fallacy. The holistic fallacy is that erroneous assumption which says that the whole is nothing more than the sum of its parts. Jung makes this mistake over and over again. He believes that the self is the fundamental and ultimate reality in the cosmos. When the self realizes itself and is whole and healthy, then man is capable of taking his place in a responsible and mature manner within society. Jung's psychology intends, as he himself says, that the self should know as a direct inner experience "what keeps the world together at its innermost center." The self becomes the agent for holding the complexities of the world together. But it is not simply an ordinary self, it is the self which recognizes the One, the All, the God, the Christ, and perhaps even the Buddha within itself. It is the self which is capable of transcending all of the insoluble problems of the world by a higher illumination of a more unified consciousness.

Jung affirms that the individual personality is the basic element of culture. "Only he who can deliberately say 'Yes' to the power of the destiny he finds within himself becomes a personality," and only such a personality is able to find a real place within a collective; only such a personality can form a community to become an integral part of a group of human beings.[55] The self-realized individual recognizes his uniqueness within the whole: "An actual conflict with the collective norm takes place only when an individual way is raised to a norm, which, moreover, is the fundamental aim of extreme individualism."[56] Self-realization means that with regard to one's fellow man one is kind and tolerant, and one is able to be so because of the conscious experience of one's own darkest depths:

> In as much as collectives are mere accumulations of individuals, their problems are also accumulations of individual problems. . . . Such problems are solved only by a general change of attitude. . . . It [the change] begins with a change in the individual himself. It will continue as a transformation of the individual's personal likes and dislikes, of his outlooks on life and of his values, and only the accumulation of such individual changes will produce a collective solution.[57]

And there is the holistic fallacy in its starkest form. What is needed to change collective behavior is psychologically healthy members of that collective. You need a kind of resident psychiatrist for every collective; and if he is successful with his patients, the result will be a collective that functions in a healthy way! But that is an absolutely absurd position, simplistic in its naivete and completely foreign to the empirical facts. And it is Jung who constantly reminds his readers that his approach to the psyche is empirical and therefore scientific. He should have known better if he were at all sensitive to the psychological behavior of his compatriots during the two great wars. He would have known then that collectives or communities do not function according to the wills of their members.

Jung is flatly and dangerously wrong for two reasons. First, collective behavior is qualitatively different from individual behavior.

55. Jung, *Integration of the Personality,* p. 287.
56. Jung, *Psychological Types,* p. 563.
57. Jung, *Psychology and Religion,* p. 95.

Group mores have a complexity all their own, and they overcome the value stances and *Weltanschauung* of the individual members of the collective. Man may achieve an integration of the self which is functional for him in his private life. But there is no relationship between that individual self and the self which is part of a collective. There, collective norms determine behavior. The objectives of the group override and overwhelm the objectives of the individual. And that is probably why the great prophets have never been part of collectives and why saints and martyrs are the first to be sacrificed.

I hesitate to make the following proposition, but the longer I think about it, the more I am convinced that it is correct. Psychic wholeness does not necessarily contribute to rational collective behavior. There have been many psychologically healthy individuals who have started wars and who have initiated racial strife. The fact that they were psychologically whole may have meant that they were capable of ever greater suppression and barbarism. That is, of course, the lesson behind the failures of the Moral Rearmament Movement and other kinds of similar organizations whose purpose is to edify spiritually whole groups of people. Groups have behavioral norms all their own. There are laws which pertain to collective activity which are absolutely different from individual behavior. Norman O. Brown, in *Love's Body,* does not recognize this fact. He writes: "Then the body of the Enlightened One becomes luminous in appearance, convincing and inspiring by its mere presence, while every word and every gesture, and even his silence, communicate the overwhelming reality of the Dharma."[58] But that fundamentally Jungian notion of the impact of personality upon the collective simply does not work. No symbolic interpretation of man's place in society can remove the impact of centuries of deception and exploitation that have forced some men to be subservient to other men. What the psychologist must accomplish is to subvert the established meaning of man and society, but he must do so literally, not simply symbolically. Only then can he translate the impossible into the possible, the mystical into the real, the metaphysical utopia into a historical one.

Jung does not have a notion of sin, of man's radical separation from

58. Norman O. Brown, *Love's Body* (New York: Random House, 1966).

God or from whatever principle or power is the source of his redemption. Jung believes that analysis can help to overcome the divisions within man's basic nature. Man can be led scientifically and clinically to the point where the laws of the psyche remove separation, hostility, differentiation, jealousy, perversion, and the like. But again, Jung's system is on the side of the angels. He does not describe ordinary human beings as they are empirically sensitized, even those beings whose archetypes have been revealed to consciousness. Man is selfish and egotistical. That is a fact of human life. His enormous propensity for self-survival far outweighs his acquired altruistic nature. Man cannot be psychoanalyzed to personal wholeness, psychic or otherwise. Wholeness can come about solely through an act of grace by the ultimate source and ground of man's being. And that being men usually call God!

2. THE IMPLICIT MYSTICISM IN JUNG'S PSYCHOLOGY

The basic theological problem in Jung's analytic psychology is its implicit mysticism. I am permitted to speak of theological problems in Jung's psychology because he himself speaks of his psychology as a redemptive spiritual gestalt.

Depth psychologies must of necessity deal with abstractions, paradoxes, linguistic imprecision, and scientifically unverifiable hypotheses. The reason for this is simply that the discipline is involved structurally in an area of experience which is noncognitive and spiritual. The mystic's language and experience perhaps best suit the needs of the psychologist as he attempts to explain what he is about. Jung wants to avoid metaphysical constructs because they impose artificial structures on the kinds of psychic experience that he discovers. He can speak of the "transcendence of problems," which for him means that a problem cannot be resolved, but can only be experienced, and experienced in such a way as to provide the content for a systematic analysis. And Jung must also dodge the logical construct because his realm of experience is one not congruent with neat intellectual order; he takes his experiences where he finds them!

But problems for theology emerge once Jung discovers that the wholeness of personality emerges from within the individual psyche itself. As soon as you affirm this thesis, you immediately detract from the theological claims of the Jewish and Christian faiths. What both Judaism and Christianity affirm is the historic objectivity of biblical events, events which constitute for the believer the source of his salvation, that is, of man's total spiritual and psychic wholeness. What Jung has done is to reduce the historical fact of the biblical events to an extension and deepening of consciousness. Now he can do this only at great risk to the biblical events of Exodus and Resurrection. What he does is to make those events symbols of man's psychic unity. But they cannot have any independent reality over against their psychic appropriation. And for that reason, the kingdom of God is always within you. The way of individuation is always the way of the self realizing its own possibilities. Then and only then can you claim that the All, the One, the immanent God has been born within the soul. Jung puts it in clear and unequivocal terms: "The psychological fact that has the greatest power in a man acts as God, because it is always the overwhelming psychic factor that is called God."[59] Jung can speak about a reciprocal relationship between God and man, but what he really means is that "on the one hand one can conceive man as a function of God and, on the other, God as a psychological function of man."[60] What that means is that God is immanent within the soul. "I live, yet not I, but Christ lives in me" is a biblical expression which Jung interprets as the feeling that the individual has of being a child of God. But it is a psychic fact and is only an experience of the self. Or then we can call it by another name—the Tao, Buddhahood, the All Encompassing One, Om, or Mana. Whatever is the principle of psychic wholeness, it is within the psyche. "It is the soul that makes metaphysical assertions from its inborn divine creative power"; the soul posits the differences between the metaphysical essences. "It is not merely the condition of metaphysical reality, it is metaphysical reality."[61] Now Jung does not want to use the term metaphysical because he really means psychological, even though the way of individuation appears to rest upon fundamental metaphysical assump-

59. Jung, *Psychology and Religion,* p. 146.

60. Jung, *Psychological Types,* p. 340.

61. Introduction to *Das tibetanisch Totenbuch,* p. 19, from J. Goldbrunner, *Individuation,* p. 170.

tions about man's place in the universe. Jung refers to psychic health as influencing man's *Weltanschauung.* The archetypes obey hidden supraempirical laws, internal to themselves. But Jung insists that he is rejecting metaphysical assumptions and cannot offer any intelligent reason for their existence except that the archetypes appear in the psychic experiences of man. But then he likens the way of individuation and the concomitant experiences to Kant's *Ding an sich,* which for Jung is not a metaphysical construct, but a "negative border-line" concept, a possible experience of the known and not the unknown. So he has it both ways: the psychic and the metaphysical merge into one reality, the individuated self, which is not simply a datum of empirical observation but is also a postulate of metaphysical speculation.

3. THE TRUTH CLAIMS OF THE WORLD'S RELIGIONS

For Jung, the various world religions give information about the mysteries of the soul. They are symbolic expressions of the process of individuation and lack any and all qualities of what Jews and Christians mean by revelation. Religion is transformed into symbolic psychology! But no more. The events of the biblical revelation can never be more than symbolically appropriated. And if they offer health, they do so only in internal and spiritual ways. But what Jung has not made explicitly clear is that the process of individuation which he describes is found already within the Christian faith tradition. It is specifically the Christian mystical tradition, represented most characteristically by Meister Eckhardt, that he holds up as normative for the Christian experience, but to do so is incorrect and inadequate to the rich diversity of experiences possible within the Christian faith tradition.

For Jung, all religions are equally true, although restricted to particular national groupings. Race, nation, and culture are different vessels in which divine truths assume different forms. But then divinity is dependent upon psyche! And by so doing, Jung has produced a tantalizing psychologism, a classic representation of a reductionism in which the entire structure of Jewish and Christian revelation is reduced to a particular psychic experience.

It is then not without reason that Jung appreciates the Eastern philosophers so much. "I suspect them of being symbolic psychologists," he writes.[62] The idea of God is present everywhere. And if God is not consciously known, he can be known unconsciously because he can function as an archetype. But in this way God is dependent upon the enlightened consciousness, the kind of consciousness that the Eastern philosophies attempt to inspire in man.

The Church comes in for the greatest amount of criticism by Jung. The total life of the collective unconscious has been absorbed into the dogmatic archetypes of the Church, Jung claims. It was not speculative philosophy that created Christianity but an elemental spiritual need of the masses who were vegetating in the darkness. The Christian faith is that symbolic attempt to provide unity to the collective unconscious. "My attitude to all religions is therefore a positive one," Jung writes:

> In their teachings I recognize the figures which I have met in my patients' dreams and fantasies. In their morals I see the same or similar attempts which my patients make from their own invention or inspiration to find the right way to deal with the powers of the soul. The sacred rites, the ritual, the initiations and asceticism are extremely interesting to me as constantly changing and formally varied techniques of producing the right way.[63]

Man, therefore, invented the techniques and passed them on from generation to generation. The various historic religions are therefore an expression of humanity's collective experience. The language of religion is symbolic. The symbol is made up of the two sides of the psyche, the conscious and the unconscious. As an expression of the unconscious it is a translation of its primitive and archaic elements into consciousness. As an expression of consciousness, it is an expression of man's spiritual achievement. The two come together symbolically in the soul. But only in the soul. There is no corresponding objective reality to the psychological unity.

As noted earlier, Jung wants to avoid metaphysical statements:

62. C. G. Jung, Introduction to *The Secret of the Golden Flower* (A Chinese Book of Life), trans. C. F. Baynes (London: Routledge, 1931), p. 128.

63. C. G. Jung, *The Practice of Psychotherapy,* from The Collected Works, Vol. 16 (New York: Pantheon Books, 1968–), pp. 36ff.

Every pronouncement about the transcendent should be avoided, for it is always only a ridiculous presumption of the human psyche unaware of its limitations. When, therefore, God or *Tao* is called an impulse or state of the mind, then something is said *only* about the *knowable, not* however, about the unknowable, concerning which nothing at all can be ascertained.[64]

God is an archetype only as a type in the psyche. Jung posits nothing positive or negative about the existence of God. The archetype of hero does not prove the factual existence of a hero. "As the eye to the sun, so the soul corresponds to God . . . at all events the soul must contain in itself the faculty of relation to God." But only the faculty! The psyche corresponds then to the God image. It has the capacity to grasp the God image through psychic means. More than that Jung refuses to admit. "The religious point of view understands the imprint as the working of an imprinter; the scientific point of view understands it as the symbol of an unknown and incomprehensible content."[65] Psychologically, the process of individuation leads the individual to knowledge of the unknown through an inner experience, whose validity is affirmed only by the individual who has experienced the unknown. And by so doing, Jung has led us to the shaky shores of Gnosticism, or knowledge of the divine by private means!

64. C. G. J,ung, Introduction to *The Secret of the Golden Flower* (A Chinese Book of Life), p. 135.
65. C. G. Jung, *Psychology and Alchemy,* pp. 13,15; quoted in Jacobi, *Psychology of C. G. Jung,* p. 197.

CONCLUSION

TOWARDS A POSITIVE
THEOLOGICAL STATEMENT
ON TRANSCENDENCE

I have attempted to demonstrate in this book that the search for transcendence is a search undertaken by theorists from many disciplines. What I believe is most characteristic of the preceding analysis is that the search for transcendence is an endeavor which takes place within nontheological intellectual communities. Culture analysts, political theorists, Marxist philosophers, psychoanalysts, scientists of the psyche, and others who probe the content of human consciousness and the dimensions of human society have worked diligently to define the concept of transcendence. Transcendence, when characterized as personal liberation (Reich), as the possibility of historical alternatives (Marcuse), as *creatio ex nihilo* (Laing), as future (Bloch), and as self-realization (Jung) are all illustrative of the attempts by theorists within several scientific disciplines to construct a concept akin to the Jewish and Christian notion of transcendence. The extraordinary nature of the search for transcendence, when undertaken from a nontheological starting point, is that the intelligibility and authenticity of the discipline, whether it be by a social, political, or psychoanalytic theorist, are never abrogated. The search for transcendence is a bona fide intellectual pursuit and is not one about which Jewish and Christian theologians ought to be apologetic.

The consequences for the theological enterprise are thereby obvious.

1. This-worldly transcendence, or the rejection of the immanentist point of view, that point of view which affirms that all of the condi-

tions for the total fulfillment of life are present within the human situation, is affirmed by the theologian and the nontheologian alike. The social, political, and psychoanalytic theorists, in league with Jewish and Christian theologians, acknowledge that human life is not all that it can be, and together they attempt to devise ways to bring about total human fulfillment, using the categories appropriate to their individual scientific disciplines. To do so is to acknowledge from many different points of view that the desire for wholeness is a basic human characteristic. Transcendence, as defined in the different ways by the representative thinkers in this book, shares a common theme, and that is that it intends total life fulfillment, or redemption and reconciliation. Transcendence means therefore the concrete resolution of social, economic, and political problems as well as spiritual and psychic wholeness. Transcendence becomes, in fact, a general category, utilized by many diverse disciplines to mean essentially the same thing, that is, the total fulfillment of human life. The theologian, then, when he speaks of transcendence in a this-worldly manner, shares the same moral objectives as the humanistic and social sciences. He is not describing a world foreign to the ordinary experiences of the common man, a world "up there" inhabited by divine and supernatural beings. He is pointing to a fundamental human drive, that urge within man for the enhancement and completion of human personality, the amelioration of those tensions and differences within his world that inhibit the perfect fulfillment of the human condition.

What I believe is particularly relevant about the preceding investigation is that I think I have demonstrated the convergence of the theological and the nontheological disciplines on one essential point, that of the human need for health and wholeness. Whatever may be the definition of transcendence given by the different social and political and psychoanalytic theorists, the objective is always the same, to bring into being that which the human condition demands, that is, the perfection of being. And it is just that objective which Jews and Christians have intended with their affirmations about the being of God and the nature of his activity in human history.

Of course, one cannot claim that theology has a more valid concept of transcendence than the other disciplines, because the claims of theology must also be empirically verified; one can say it is evident that theology is not an irrelevant and antihumanistic discipline. Rather, it appears to me that theology has entered the intellectual arena once again with great vitality and forcefulness, and it does so claiming to be an accurate interpreter of the human condition. But even more so, theology asserts that it can provide an adequate resolution to the human dilemma, the inherent desire of man for wholeness and perfection.

2. The search for transcendence demonstrates that the critical issue for the theologian is not to attempt a description of the nature and being of God but instead to attempt an exposition of the consequences of God's activity in human history. What I am suggesting is that when the Jew and Christian affirm faith in transcendence and when they specifically mean faith in the transcendent God of the Old and New Testaments, they are affirming faith in the God who has acted in human history to redeem man from his sins. That affirmation, when translated into categories congruent with the humanistic objectives of the social sciences, refers specifically to the effect that the revelation of God has had upon human life. When that translation has been made, transcendence becomes a historical, and not a metaphysical, category. Transcendence refers to the transformation the sovereign and eternal God has effected upon the concrete human situation in terms of reconciliation, redemption, the restoration of health, the amelioration of social and political divisions, and so on. Transcendence must be grasped, not as it has so often been in the past, in spatial terms, referring to the God up there, beyond the affairs of human life, but specifically in terms of what God has effected historically on behalf of man. I want to suggest that we might not want to think of transcendence as a category at all. Transcendence is not the description of the inner metaphysical being of God, but transcendence refers to an event, that historical event reported in the Old and New Testaments, which brings about the restoration of health, that is, reconciliation, to man and society.

The history of Christian thought demonstrates the debilitating effect that the category of transcendence has had upon the development of a vital and appealing humanism. To employ spatial metaphors which shift the location of transcendence from "out there" to "the depth of being" continues to subject the notion of transcendence to the criticism that God, or the ultimate reality, is distinct from and uncaring for the welfare of concrete historical man. What I am suggesting is that transcendence has little to do with the nature and attributes of God but has everything to do with the consequence of God's activity in history, that is, to introduce a transcendent dimension to human life.

That transcendent dimension of which the theologian speaks can be described by reference to concrete indices of what it means to be human. The theologian cannot content himself by speaking in abstract generalities about the nature of human life. When the theologian argues that human life has been enhanced by the revelation of God in history, he means something quite specific about the quality of that human life. And the quality of human life refers specifically to empirical indices of the content of that life. The redemption of man from sin, which event has been effected by God's revelation of himself in history, means concretely that human life has been given a quality of existence that it did not previously have. When the translation has been made from theological categories to humanistic ones, that quality of existence describes human life in social, political, economic, and psychoanalytic terms. Martin Luther, in *A Treatise on Christian Liberty*, anticipated a great many of the descriptive categories of the humanist when he described the grace offered to neighbor which flows from the experienced grace of God:

> From faith flows love and joy in the Lord, and from love a joyful, willing and free mind that serves one's neighbor willingly and takes no account of gratitude or ingratitude, of praise or blame, of gain or loss. For a man does not serve that he may put men under obligations, he does not distinguish between friends and enemies, nor does he anticipate their thankfulness or unthankfulness, but most freely and willingly he spends himself and all that he has, whether he wastes all on the thankless or whether he gains a reward. . . . As our heavenly father has in Christ freely come to our help, we also ought freely to help our neighbor through our body and its works, and each should become as it were a Christ to the other, that we may be Christs to one another and Christ may be the same in all.[1]

1. *Works of Martin Luther*, intro. by Henry Eyster Jacobs (Philadelphia: Muhlenberg Press, 1943), p. 338.

The theological description of the redeemed life affirms "a joyful, willing and free mind," the willful service of the neighbor, the rejection of such criteria for action as "gratitude or ingratitude, . . . praise or blame, . . . gain or loss." The man of faith does not put another man "under obligation," nor does he "distinguish between friends and enemies" when he serves man. He spends himself and is not devastated by the lack of return for his services. Nor is he prompted to serve because he anticipates a reward.

Human life is radically altered, in empirically measured ways, by the revelation of the transcendent God in human history.

3. Transcendence is defined by the nontheological interpreters in this volume in such a way as to emphasize two of its essential component parts: first, transcendence defined in psychic or spiritual terms as wholeness and health; second, transcendence defined in political or social terms as historical purpose and direction. Reich, Marcuse, Laing, Bloch, and Jung all pay allegiance to the profoundest of psychological and political insights by their diligent search for a definition of transcendence.

The theologian can profit from the discoveries of the psychological and political implications of the meaning of transcendence. The theologian does not introduce nonrelevant concepts to the meaning he gives to transcendence, nor does he discover factors that do not exist there; but he ought to be conscious that the concept of transcendence has a psychological and political dimension. "God's in his heaven, all's right with the world" is an old bromide, but when viewed from the perspective of the theologian seeking for wisdom from the social scientist, it becomes the occasion for asking the question, What are the psychological and political indications that the world is "all right"? What I want to suggest is that the theological search for those kinds of analytic allegiances which will enhance his own conceptual task and will enable him to flesh out and give meaning to his own categories. He will then become aware of the deepest spiritual meaning of transcendence (cf. Reich, Laing, and Jung) and of the broadest political implications (cf. Marcuse and Bloch). For the sake of clarity, we may designate these two dimensions of transcendence as self-transcendence and historical transcendence. This is at the point where we may begin to speak of the interrelatedness of individual wholeness and social responsibility. The relationship of the individual to transcendence is always more profound when it includes the social-political dimension and introduces the individual to the struggle to transform community than when it defines that relationship solely in spiritual and individualistic ways. Any dichotomy between self-transcendence and historical transcendence is false in theory and perverse in practice and, moreover, is foreign to the Jewish and Christian witnesses to the redemptive action of God in history. And ultimately what transcendence means is the absolute transformation of every part of the human experience, individual and social, by the redemptive activity of the sovereign and transcendent God, who becomes identified with man in order to effect wholeness.

I would like to conclude this book with a quotation from the theologian Edward LeRoy Long, Jr., who has captured succinctly the essence of what it means empirically to live within the dimension of transcendence and to affirm on the one hand the overriding availability of grace and the corresponding response of responsible stewardship of that grace:

> Life lived in response to God consists of holding many lesser loyalties in subordination to one ultimate and commanding devotion—not in order that the lesser loyalties be spurned but in order to embrace them in a more sustained and sustaining framework of meaning. The primacy of the ultimate trust as conceived in Biblical faith is consistent with human devotion to lesser causes unless and until such devotion makes the lesser causes into rival absolutes. Man's devotion to God is not diminished by his attempted conquest of nature as long as such conquest is undertaken in recognition of man's final dependence upon the Creator; man's devotion to God is not diminished by his acceptance of political responsibility unless such political responsibility is embraced as a substitute trust for the God who acts providentially in history; even coercive struggle may be a legitimate means of service unless it becomes a source of devotion to an earthly crusade and admits to no judgment or criticism of itself. The doctrines of Creation and of Providence preserve radical monotheism compatible with man's embrace of life in this world.[2]

2. Edward LeRoy Long, Jr., *The Role of the Self in Conflicts and Struggle* (Philadelphia: Westminster Press, 1962), p. 143.

INDEX

Abzon /antwalin p.66